P9-CAE-405

Beyond National Borders

Reflections on Japan and the World

Beyond National Borders

Reflections on Japan and the World

Kenichi Ohmae

DOW JONES-IRWIN
Homewood, Illinois   60430

© Kenichi Ohmae, 1987

All rights reserved. No part of this publication may be
reproduced, stored in a retrieval system, or transmitted,
in any form or by any means, electronic, mechanical,
photocopying, recording, or otherwise, without the prior
written permission of the copyright holder.

This publication is designed to provide accurate and
authoritative information in regard to the subject matter
covered. It is sold with the understanding that the copyright
holder is not engaged in rendering legal, accounting, or
other professional service. If legal advice or other expert
assistance is required, the services of a competent
professional person should be sought.

*From a Declaration of Principles jointly adopted by a Committee
of the American Bar Association and a Committee of Publishers.*

13-2447-01   ISBN 1-55623-017-6

Library of Congress Catalog Card No. 86–72864

Printed in the United States of America

1 2 3 4 5 6 7 8 9 0 MP 4 3 2 1 0 9 8 7

*To my Mother, Sumiko, and
late Father, Tadao.*

I have written over a dozen books in Japanese and a few books in English. Normally I do not try to translate my Japanese books into English, because Western readers expect structured, well-supported arguments. Most Japanese readers would find this kind of book mechanical and lacking in insight. They like books, even in business and nonfiction categories, to be more impressionistic and inspirational.

Despite this problem, I decided to translate a book I published in Japanese in January 1986, entitled *Now that I have seen the world, I can see Japan better.* Over the past several years, I had written in magazines and newspapers on various subjects outside of my professional concerns as a consultant to corporate management in the United States, Europe and Asian Newly Industrial Countries, and Japan. My subjects included Japan–U.S. trade problems, exchange rates, social value systems, land reforms, Southeast Asia, and education. I wanted for some time to pull them together and consider their implications for Japan. I felt my American education (at MIT), and marriage to an American woman, and my travels and work for over a decade as a partner in a truly multinational organization, gave me a unique perspective worth conveying to my countrymen.

Until recently, however, I was convinced that what I had to say would be misinterpreted by fellow Japanese. In certain respects, I would be severely critical of my country. So it was with some fear that finally, during the latter part of 1985 as the trade "wars" worsened, I put my arguments on paper. But when the book came out, it was received very well. In fact, its sales of 200,000 copies so far (as of October 1986) have been much better than my publisher and I could have expected. The reactions of readers and critics of the book were almost all positive. Of the 2,000 readers who sent me letters, only a half dozen really disagreed with what I had to say. A majority of them said, "If you are right (and I believe you are), then our journalists, politicians, and intellectuals have not been telling us what we need to hear." I am delighted that the intention of this book, an honest self-appraisal, has been positively accepted by my fellow countrymen. I am beginning to see some hope for our ability to change in a fundamental way.

Like others around the world, many of us in Japan are victims of our upbringing, generally held perceptions, and what the government says. We may be entering the age of information, but it is far from perfect and balanced information.

There is a great deal of misunderstanding about international economics. I remember learning in high school of a particular glass tube with different "chimneys," the bottoms of which were all connected. Pour water in any one of these chimneys and the level of water in all of them becomes the same, regardless of their shapes. Modern countries are interconnected like this tube. In different countries similar standards of living are emerging that tend to create people with the same consumption patterns and value systems. As a result, a more or less natural distribution of human capital and technological resources across national borders is taking place. For example, a good product will find markets in all key countries of the world, penetrating equally into their households. Similarly, excess cash will find different homes until investment opportunities are equalized.

Yet governments, acting only within their relevant geographical boundaries, are increasingly getting in the way of this redistribution. Part of the reason is that almost all modern democracies, sadly, are overly sensitive to special interest groups. If our governments were based on what a majority of people wanted, we would today see American rice being imported into Japan, and more Japanese semiconductor chips sailing to America, because that, in the end, would make both products cheaper for most consumers. Yet both are regulated or restricted because of special interests.

The politics of nationalism inevitably intrude on free trade. When there is a trade imbalance between two states, say between California and Arizona, there is no national outcry about lost jobs, unfair trade barriers, or dumping. But when the products cross national borders, then companies and other interests can mobilize political powers. Suddenly consumers, who otherwise would have benefited from foreign products, become nationalistic. I see this happen again and again in Japan for products as varied as beef and chemicals. It happens in other countries as well. We need a better understanding of the mechanisms and misperceptions by which special interest opinion prevails as well as the dangers associated with synthetic nationalism. Without this understanding, we cannot hope to solve the problems now threatening the free world.

I am deeply concerned about the misperceptions shared by many of my countrymen. That was the primary reason I have written this book to my fellow Japanese. Japan must grow up. It must abandon its long history and mind-set of an isolated island nation in order to become a truly global citizen.

My McKinsey colleagues in the United States encouraged me to undertake a translation because they thought Americans needed to hear what would have been a private conversation. I did not rewrite the book for an American audience, because there are many more qualified authors to write on what Americans need to do to enhance the role of the United States in a global economy. I did try to give it a little more structure than it has in the Japanese edition and added materials to clarify the points I wanted to make. I've also added new examples and reflected recent events to bolster my arguments. My hope is that Americans will understand as a result of reading this book what kind of soul-searching we in Japan are going through, because we are genuinely concerned and unsure about how to improve our relationships with the rest of the world, particularly with the United States, and want to grow as a respected member of the global economy. And maybe what I have to say will also cause some Americans to ask why U.S. scholars and politicians haven't been telling people what they ought to know.

I should express my appreciation to my colleagues at McKinsey & Company. And in particular, thanks are due to Bill Matassoni, Vice President of Communications at McKinsey, and Tim Ferguson, Contributions Editor of *The Wall Street Journal*.

Kenichi Ohmae

CONTENTS _____

The Wealth of Japan: A Reappraisal

The key to a nation's future is its human resources. It used to be its natural resources, but not any more. The quality and number of its educated people now determines a country's likely prosperity or decline.

Japan, with its 120 million well-educated and hardworking people, is better endowed with the resources vital to success than any other nation in the world.

Forty years ago, Japan had a population of roughly 100 million, and no task was as urgent as feeding its people. We had to work terribly hard, night and day, just to get enough to eat. Japan's population back in those days was a burden, not an asset. Not only were they unable to produce wealth: they consumed it. They were a drain on the nation, not a resource.

But thanks to the passion of the Japanese for self-improvement and the interest of Japanese mothers in their children's education, the educational level of the average Japanese is virtually unrivaled today. Even more important, the size of Japan's population is itself a great resource and asset, enabling Japan to create greater wealth for its people and the world.

IS MINERAL WEALTH A HANDICAP?

In contrast to Japan, countries rich in natural resources are suffering economic setbacks. The members of OPEC and mineral-rich nations now realize that their oil and ores are not enough to prime and fuel economic growth. Many of the Arab countries have built, or half built, port facilities, universities, public office buildings, and the like, paying little attention to the overall balance of their infrastructures. Sadly, they don't seem to have made much progress toward creating the sort of industries that will still be producing wealth when the wells run dry. On top of it all, oil prices are falling, forcing the Arabs to slow down the pace of construction.

There are other examples of countries rich in natural resources, but still not wealthy. Australia has yet to pull out of a five-year-long recession, and its economic growth rate has been lower than England's for a century, according to my McKinsey partner in Sydney, Fred Hilmer.[1] Indonesia trails its resourceless neighbors—Singapore, Taiwan, and Korea—and its per capita gross national product is less than one tenth of Japan's.

Even the United States, a nation possessing every kind of natural resource from agriculture to oil and uranium, is now a net debtor.

AND THE POOR SHALL INHERIT THE INFORMATION AGE

Japan's position is exactly the opposite. For the past hundred years, Japan has been constantly aware of its lot as a poor cousin. It has tried to make up for its mineral poverty in many ways. One was to equip "a strong army to build a strong nation." As we all know, its attempt to lay hold of overseas resources militarily led to crushing defeat in World War II.

After the war, Japan's motto was rewritten. Building up an economy based on trade in manufactured goods became the credo of the primary school curriculum. In virtually all textbooks, a litany of economic necessity was (and still is) preached. "Japan is a small island country with few natural resources. Eighty percent of its territory is mountainous, and 100 million people live crowded together on the small remaining flat areas. It must import raw materials from overseas, use them to manufacture value-added products, and export these products in order to buy food to eat. In no other way will Japan be able to survive. Those who don't work can't eat."

---

[1]Frederick G. Hilmer, *When the Luck Runs Out* (Sydney, Australia: Harper & Row, 1985).

Perhaps at no other time in history have so many people all embraced such a clear definition of the economic underpinnings of their society. Ask any Japanese to describe his country and he will deliver the same stock phrases about tiny Japan's paucity of resources, using almost the same words in the same order. Anyone who has had to deal with the Japanese has heard it repeated countless times.

WE DON'T EVEN KNOW HOW MUCH WATER WE HAVE

The lesson has been so well learned that it colors Japanese perceptions of many events. Consider the recent extension of sovereignty over coastal areas to 200 nautical miles. The Japanese public was unanimously against the idea, fearing that Japanese boats would be shut out of the world's fishing grounds and unable to catch enough to feed them.

No one realized that by the extension of sovereignty around its many islands, Japan had become the seventh largest nation in the world, with an area of 4.5 million square kilometers. Nor did anyone celebrate the fact that Japan began to net fully 60 percent of its total catch of 10 million tons in waters under its direct control. This and the fact that fish are being increasingly farmed, not caught, are reasons why Japan is unlikely to suffer much from decreasing dependence on operations in foreign waters. Yet statements by fishing interests opposed to the 200 nautical mile limit are believed by most Japanese to express a legitimate grievance, and provoke anxiety about the future supply of fish. Most Japanese considered the change to be a monumental defeat of the Japanese diplomacy.

Thus, whether or not Japan is actually tiny and resourceless, its attitudes and behavior are affected by the belief that it is so. Japan associates openly with the Arab countries, but not with Israel. It views Korea and Taiwan as rivals, and courts Indonesia and Malaysia. It gives aid to the Philippines and Thailand as if they were neither rivals nor worth courting seriously and aid alone were more than enough.

Japan's classification of the world's countries is the natural outcome of its own self-image. Just mention Brazil and China and eyes light up, but talk about India and Argentina and you will elicit only shrugs. The Japanese divide the world into two types: resource-rich countries that promise to alleviate Japan's mineral poverty, and consumer countries that provide markets for manufactured products.

Japanese simply don't care about the rest of the world. Perhaps our single-minded and arrogant view would be understandable if Japan were truly a tiny nation, fighting against terrible odds just to survive. But it is not any longer. Tiny, weak Japan is a myth. And the world has shared our belief in this myth until recently.

A MODEL FOR THE JAPANESE: THE SWISS

Today, the basis of the world's wealth is shifting from natural resources to advanced technology. The natural resource superpowers are watching the relative worth of their assets dwindle while nations with intelligent human resources are expanding their trade and accumulating surpluses.

Switzerland, with neither natural resources nor former colonies, continues to have trade surpluses—even with Japan. Thanks to its highly educated and well-trained people, Switzerland's three largest banks continue to enjoy considerable success in the world's financial markets, and Swiss firms have profitable manufacturing operations in every advanced industrial nation.

Swiss-based multinationals are present and very active, directly and indirectly, in the Japanese market. They have made Nestlé, Ciba-Geigy, Hoffmann-La Roche, Sandoz, Sulzer, Brown Boveri, Knorr, and Maggi familiar corporate and household words in Japan. They have managed to enter the market and thrive, belying loud claims by firms from the rest of the world that Japan is impenetrable. But unlike Japanese multinationals abroad, they are hardly noticeable as a "foreign" company. They are quietly successful.

Compared to tiny Switzerland, with only six million people, Japan is a human resource giant, with 20 times the population resources. If Japan succeeds in maintaining or raising its people's education and skills to the same level as the Swiss, its strength will become even greater. And if Japanese firms undergo the same sort of quiet transformation into multinationals as Swiss firms have, Japan bashing and trade friction will be significantly alleviated. A new chapter will have to be written in the history of Japanese relations with the world. Japan will have grown up.

ON A PAR WITH THE UNITED STATES

The population of the United States is now twice that of Japan, but both have a roughly equal number of engineers. The United States has a higher illiteracy rate and more citizens on welfare. And attitudes toward compulsory education, although harder to measure, are certainly not as strong in the United States as in Japan. Just look at how many Americans leave high school without being able to do simple algebra.

A recent study published in *Science* magazine pointed out that American children in kindergarten, first, and fifth grade lag considerably behind Japanese children in math—a key to keeping the United States ahead in science and technology. For example, of the 100 children who did best on the fifth-grade tests, only one was an American.

The study's authors noted that American children attend school an average of 178 days a year. The Japanese school year consists of 240 days and the school day there is an hour longer. The authors also said that Japanese children spend a lot more time at the computer than they do on the playground.

And the commitment to technically oriented education extends across the board. Japan graduates 75,000 engineers a year—3,000 more than the United States—from a university student population one fifth the size of the United States.[2]

An article in *The Wall Street Journal* pointed out that American students scored just above their counterparts in Swaziland on standardized tests.[3] There are other comparisons. Recently, Adam Smith noted in an article in *Esquire*:

The Japanese have nearly 100 percent literacy; we do not, by a long shot. They graduate more students from high school than we

---

[2]Robert McCurry (Senior Vice President, Toyota Motor Sales, U.S.A.), "Competing with Japan" (Delivered before the Commonwealth Club, San Francisco, Calif., May 9, 1986). Reprinted in *Vital Speeches*, July 15, 1986, pp. 593–96.

[3]John Saxon, "Classroom Calculators Add to Math Illiteracy," *The Wall Street Journal*, May 16, 1986, p. 24.

do (90 versus 75 percent), and they are in many ways far better prepared—they have had several years more of math and science and foreign languages. Japanese teachers are more highly paid than ours; it is the extracurricular programs and physical plants that are inferior. American students have long vacations, teaching is less of a prestige profession, and American families, being less coherent than Japanese families at the moment, are not as demanding of their schools. In the opinion of some educators, the average Japanese 18-year-old is on a par with the average American college graduate.[4]

As go the children, so go the adults. The Educational Testing Service in the United States recently surveyed 3,600 people in their early 20s. Reports *The Economist* magazine:

> In posing "real-world tasks" instead of multiple choice questions, the survey reveals an alarming proportion of the allegedly literate unable to decipher the signposts of everyday life.

> Only 38 percent of the sample could find the cost of a two-item lunch on a menu, for example, including only 60 percent of college graduates and 8 percent of blacks. Only 20 percent could read a long-distance bus schedule, including only 40 percent of college graduates and under 3 percent of blacks. Taking the literacy yardstick of an eighth-grade (age 13–14) reading level, 47 percent of blacks, 29 percent of Hispanics, and 15 percent of whites fall short.[5]

In America it is apparently possible to earn a high school or even college diploma and still not be able to read a map or menu.

There is such a difference in productivity between our educational systems, at least until recently, that despite the fact that there are twice as many people in America, we might even have an equivalent quantity of human resources, at least the kind needed by an economy determined to master advanced information sciences and high technology. Japan's new supercreditor status, its recent technological trade surpluses, and its continuing general trade surpluses are just precursors to what may come in the future if we can maintain our intelligent human stock. As we approach the 21st century, Japan's reserves of highly trained and educated workers will be the asset most fundamental to our ability to create wealth.

---

[4]Adam Smith, "Will Japan's Rising Sons Trade Us In?" *Esquire*, September 1986, pp. 71–72.

[5]September 27, 1986, p. 25.

JAPAN'S PROBLEM IS THE JAPANESE

There is a problem, however: the Japanese mentality. We don't realize we are sitting on a gold mine and powder keg. Though our human resource reserves have wonderful potential, we have no idea how badly foreign industries are hurt by our manufacturers. How we ignore our Asian neighbors. How much the world has come to resent us. Japan is a superpower unaware.

The Arabs once cut off the West's oil supplies. The chance, however unlikely, that Japan might some day refuse to ship machine tools to the United States is now being used by the U.S. Department of Commerce as a pretext to restrict imports. It has probably never occurred to the Japanese that we hold such power. But similar arguments are frequently heard in Europe. In fact, the threat of boycotts, however unbelievable to us, is a sort of theme song for anti-Japanese commentators. It is naive to call them "misunderstandings" when Europeans and Americans both hold the same point of view.

BOYCOTTS AND STOCKPILES: FOOD FOR THOUGHT

On the other hand, Arab nations have approached Japan recently with assurances that Japan can depend on secure supplies of oil. Further Arab boycotts, they say, are unthinkable. Do the Japanese believe them? Apparently not, because Japan stocks a 90-day supply of oil "just in case" and continues to drill wells at great expense in parts of Japan where, so far, only a little gas has been discovered.

Japan's food supply is an equally touchy subject about which we refuse to face realities. We use half of our arable land to grow rice, claiming the need for "food self-sufficiency," just in case of an "emergency." Yet, if there were an emergency, such as a boycott, oil stocks would run out in 90 days. After that there would not be any fuel to cook our mountains of hoarded, homegrown rice.

The cost is a highly segmented and inefficient rice industry. The government buys two thirds of the rice produced, subsidizing billions of its costs, yet we still pay five to six times the world price. Despite this inconsistent behavior, the Japanese beg the world to understand them. Not surprisingly, the world is more often astonished than understanding. The point is this: We don't understand ourselves.

We must now take a hard look in the mirror and think carefully about how we look to others. And our mirror must not be a wishing glass that makes Japan seem more beautiful and wonderful than it really is. Neither Marco Polo's report about the oriental El Dorado nor Ezra Vogel's *Japan as Number One* show us the way we really are.[6]

OVERSENSITIVE, EGOCENTRIC JAPAN

Normally complacent, the Japanese go to the other extreme of overaccommodation whenever criticism becomes too loud to ignore. But by then it is usually too late. The programs of the Japanese government, for example, are often drafted solely in response to foreign pressure—an example of unnecessary servility.

For example, when the United States mounted pressure on Japan to "open its markets," Prime Minister Nakasone turned in a series of "Action Programs" to the United States. No independent nation has done such a studentlike thing at another nation's gunpoint. We try too hard to calm down others' anger, rather than solve the underlying problems. When Richard Nixon visited China, it was a shock to us. But we could not simply tell Taiwan that we now recognized the mainland as China. We wanted to be friends with both—a good idea if it's possible. As a result, we allocated Haneda Airport to Taiwan's China Airlines (CAL) and the newly opened Tokyo International Airport at Narita to the mainland's CAAC, so that their planes wouldn't have to pass each other. All this to recognize that there are two Chinas. No other nation is doing this. Both CAL and CAAC use the same airport in Hong Kong, Los Angeles, and New York.

When our high school history textbooks are criticized by the Chinese and Koreans, we immediately apologize and correct the sentences to "accurately reflect" the fact that Japan did indeed "invade" China and Korea. Making the criticism disappear is much more important to us than solving the problems and/or not causing problems. In this case, as in others, we did not study the facts to counterargue, or to go one step further, to remind them that they (e.g., Koreans), too, present a distorted view of the

---

[6]Ezra F. Vogel, *Japan as Number One: Lessons for America* (Cambridge, Mass.: Harvard University Press, 1979).

Japanese in their textbooks. If we believe and have evidence that their Japanese education is misrepresentative, we should register this point of view. But that's not our way.

Efforts to reform our institutions are a good thing, of course, but Japan is a sovereign, not servile, nation. It must do what it deems necessary before outsiders exert pressure. It is time for us to be less responsive to criticism and more independently conscious of our responsibilities.

DOUBLE STANDARDS

Another problem is that we have double standards. We open our home markets slowly, but smugly preach free trade to the rest of the world. We let Nippon Telegraph and Telephone (NTT) and the "Denden Family" exercise a de facto monopoly through a captive-supplier relationship, but with a straight face we express concern that an IBM–NTT tie-up would be monopolistic.

"It's okay for us to do it, but outsiders have to watch their step" is our attitude. If the textile makers of Hokuriku start going bankrupt, we call it a crisis. But if Cleveland's steelworks close, we self-righteously call it a classic example of the failings of bottom-line oriented, shortsighted American management.

U.S. agricultural produce is now more important to the Japanese diet than rice. Nevertheless, we shrug off the worst recession for American farmers since the Great Depression as the result of a strong dollar. We simply go shopping elsewhere: in Argentina, China, or Australia. We thank the Japanese farmers who planted our rice, but why only fellow Japanese? Do foreign farmers deserve less concern simply because a trading company, not farmers, brought their produce to our tables?

Is Japan then qualified to ask the rest of the international community for understanding? We are not even aware of our own interests. Today, Japan depends on foreign countries for more than 80 percent of its energy and food. Despite this, it sympathizes with and defends only its own farmers and fishermen. Other agricultural suppliers are no more than abstract collective nouns, people without faces. We are not the only country guilty of this. The United States is too. Nevertheless, Japan should take another look in the mirror. How does Japan look to foreigners?

JAPAN IS STILL IN TRAINING FOR
WORLD LEADERSHIP

It is dangerous for Japan to assume that because it is rich, it has a duty to become a welfare state and vacation paradise on the Western European model. It must reject American demands and the advice of our own scholars to stop working so hard. Japan is an economic powerhouse precisely because it has a population of 120 million and has had a diligent, highly skilled work force. If this were not so, however, Japan would no longer enjoy its current prosperity. One hundred and twenty million loafers would just be so many mouths to feed. (It has been estimated that in the United States the direct charge that illiterates make on the economy in welfare payments, prison maintenance, and workmen's compensation is $20 billion.[7] And that figure doesn't consider lost opportunity and productivity.)

This is the fundamental difference between the human-resource powers of the future, whose intelligent population is their wealth, and the natural resource powers of the past. Just as computers run because current flows, Japan is strong because its people work. Computers cannot yet run on static.

Japan can't slack off now. It still has much to learn in terms of internationalizing its firms, opening its markets, becoming competitive with the United States, and above all, helping other nations to grow as well.

It is just beginning to learn how to behave in the world community. Very few of its people are yet able to play leading roles on the world stage. Japan's thinkers, managers, athletes, and singers are still provincials. Blossoming flowers on Japanese soil, they wilt when transplanted. Japan is an industrial giant, but has produced only four Nobel prize winners.

Now is not the time for conceit or for slackening our determination to improve ourselves. We should not think that because we dominate two manufacturing sectors—automobiles and electronics—we are the decathlon champions of the industrial Olympics. We must work harder in other fields to enable our nation to exercise sound leadership as an intelligent resource superpower in the 21st century. We must find ways to export jobs in

---

[7]Jonathan Kozal, *Illiterate America* (Garden City, N.Y.: Doubleday, 1985).

commodity and secondary manufacturing industries. We must find ways to cooperate with, not conquer, American, European, and Asian companies and markets.

AN AWKWARD AGE

Japan is at that awkward age between adolescence and adulthood. Its inability to form an accurate self-image is the greatest obstacle to its attaining maturity, for the key rite of passage in global society is acquiring the ability to view the world and oneself without bias. There is a real danger that unless we quickly succeed in weaning ourselves from our childhood illusions, we will repeat our past mistakes and be driven into self-defeating isolation.

Overadjustment is also a danger, however. In the mistaken belief that we no longer need to work, we may be tempted to make every Saturday a full-day holiday and to add to our long list of public holidays (already longer than that of any other advanced industrial nation). The British disease may set in before Japan acquires adequate stocks of social capital.

Either case would be a great loss to Japan and to the world, because Japan has a great deal to offer. Of all the conceivable goals and achievements that Japan might seek to accomplish in the next century, only one, I believe, is worthy of Japan. It is to prove that without wielding military might, by human strength and resourcefulness alone, a major global power can alleviate the earth's disparities and injustices.

Such an achievement would encourage other natural-resource-poor nations of the world to follow Japan's example. Their nation-building efforts would be helped and world peace would be strengthened.

I hope that this will happen. But it cannot happen, unless there is a change in the way the Japanese think. Now we must begin to think beyond national borders.

_____

CHAPTER ONE

Dangerous Illusions

Ethnically, the Japanese people are highly (even enviably) homogenous, thanks to centuries of isolation. But Japanese brought up in Japan are remarkably self-centered. Floods of Japanese-manufactured products have conquered world markets; Japan imports raw materials from nearly everywhere; the lifestyles, the material aspects of culture, and corporate activities in Japan have now all been internationalized. But most Japanese still focus on Japan.

The Japanese are interested in world news, yes—provided that it is connected directly with Japan. The Japanese press will report that Isao Aoki placed 61st in an American golf tournament, but say almost nothing about the winner.

An airplane crash, wherever it occurs, is reported within minutes, but Japanese concern and all coverage evaporate as soon as it is known that there were no Japanese aboard.

There is hardly a single Japanese who is even slightly interested in South Africa's political situation, which has gripped the West's attention for months. All that counts for Japan is South Africa's business.

Until recently, the Korean economy was wilting. Major firms, banks, and entire industries were losing money. The crisis was unprecedented, but the Japanese continued to feel threatened by Korea. Talk focused on when Korea would catch up with Japan, and on the damage Koreans would do to markets for Japanese goods around the world.

In sum, the Japanese are concerned only about themselves, and try to have as little as possible to do with events not directly affecting their interests. This was allowable in the past, when Japan was a country with little influence on international economic affairs. But today, Japan is a giant, and its ignorance is unacceptable.

With international ties becoming ever closer, there are few events that can be regarded as having nothing to do with Japan. What is happening in South Africa and Korea is bound to affect Japan significantly in the long run.

THE MYTH OF ECONOMIC NATIONALISM

National borders are now irrelevant to most companies and consumers, regardless of whether they are in Japan, North America, or Europe. Current frictions and clashes at the national level may seem serious, but they are insignificant at the microeconomic level where customers buy and companies sell. Americans are eager to buy Sony Walkmans and wear Benetton sweaters. Like other cosmopolitan consumers in advanced industrial countries, they acknowledge the value of good products and buy them, regardless of their country of origin. The Japanese are not aware of contributing to imports when they drink the products made by Coca-Cola, nor do they feel any duty to drink a Japanese brand instead. They have no compunctions about consuming imported products. They pay no attention to the fact (if they are aware of it) that Coca-Cola is an American company. Or that Kleenex tissues are made in Japan by a joint venture that is 50 percent American owned. Schick has the largest share of the Japanese market for razor blades, but Japanese men don't feel they have jilted the leading domestic brand.

Because consumer tastes are becoming so quickly and thoroughly cosmopolitan, they thwart efforts by governments and politicians to enhance sales by national companies. The problem is even more complicated because a company's nationality and the place where it produces goods often differ. Japanese shoe stores stock row upon row of jogging shoes—Nike, Adidas, Fila, Tiger. But few people, even avid runners, would be able to identify the nationality of the brand, let alone the country of manufacture. (For instance, Adidas is a West German firm, but in Japan it sells shoes that are made in Taiwan.)

Companies and consumers are both behaving as if they were ignorant of the national interest. And although competition among major world corporations is fierce, these companies often compete as insiders, without nationalistic flag-waving, by establishing manufacturing or marketing operations close to their customers. That is, until politics enter the picture.

When America demands that Japan open its market to American oranges, the Japanese rise up against this "unfair" demand out of pity for Japan's poor citrus farmers. At the same time, we hope that the demands will not escalate. The same is true for beef and rice.

But when it comes to our own family budgets, the reaction is quite different. If we were given the chance to buy oranges at one third and beef at one fourth the prevailing price, we would be delighted. In fact, when Japanese butchers offer "special releases" of imported beef at just a 30 percent discount, we form long lines to buy it.

Paradoxically, individuals and firms act in accordance with their own interests, but collectively are prone to nationalism, acting in conflict with these interests. Ask people if they feel so strongly about Japan's *mikan* (tangerine) farmers that they refuse to buy oranges. The answer is no. Then ask them why they are against liberalizing orange imports, and they will probably say that it would be a shame to let mikans and other native citrus fruits disappear from our tables. The problem is that we get emotional and nationalistic when we see on television that our fellow Japanese are being criticized. These emotions form our collective opinion. Nevertheless, the behavior of individual consumers— quite at odds with official public opinion—is both logical and cosmopolitan.

If the Japanese like mikans so much, there is no danger they will disappear from our tables, even if imported oranges flood our markets. There is no reason for oranges to be priced so high. If the Japanese don't like mikans enough to pay a higher price compared to the price they pay for imported oranges, then mikans ought to disappear. It should be in the final analysis the consumers' decision as to what they like to buy at what price. The problem is that consumers are not given the choice. By regulating the flow of foreign oranges, the government has made the choice that the Japanese should like expensive mikans, *and* even more expensive oranges.

To make the matter worse, these same consumers, the moment they are labeled as "the Japanese," tend to approve of the government's protectionist measure in sympathy with "the poor little mikan growers" battling against the *gigantic* American orange agribusiness enterprises.

The majority of consumers behave more rationally when it comes to opening up their wallets. That is why our exports to the United States do not go down, despite the outcries of the American government to curb Japanese imports. American people, just like the Japanese, have the same schizophrenic attitude: When it comes to personal decisions, they want the best and the cheapest regardless of the origin, but when it comes to "jobs" and their nation, they become "American."

The same inconsistency applies to the beef issue in Japan. Ask the Japanese why they are against liberalizing beef imports, and they will say that domestic livestock products must be protected. Then tell them that Japanese prices are four times as high as in the United States, and nine times as high as in Australia. Although astonished, they will immediately retort that Japanese beef tastes far better, particularly for sukiyaki, even if it costs more. This is a difficult assertion to substantiate, since the cattle are imported breeds and their feed is grown in the United States. The only factors that can explain the better taste of "Japanese" beef is the air they breathe and the water they drink. But if Japanese cattle farmers really have know-how that enables them to make beef taste better simply by supplying different air and water, why are they not exporting this miraculous animal husbandry to the rest of the world?

The cheaper the better, but no to imports. To some extent, the Japanese have been fooled by their government and industry into accepting inconvenience and inefficiency. But the real problem lies in self-delusion. The Japanese have not thought things out to their logical conclusions or taken a good, hard look at themselves.

The same could be said for Americans. They criticize Japan's markets as unfairly closed, and think that America alone stands for free trade. They forget that the access of Latin American and

Australian exports to their agricultural market is severely restricted.

They cry out that Japan has stolen their jobs, but refuse to face the facts: The United States cannot increase its international competitiveness without decreasing employment in existing industries at home. If Detroit wants to become internationally competitive (and not just with Japan), it must halve its work force and reduce pay by about 30 percent. Over time, U.S. industries have built up a bad practice by using too many people for relatively simple tasks, and have not really developed the most efficient modus operandi, taking advantage of the latest factory automation. The moment they want to modernize their plants and production methods, they will be deciding that millions of jobs will have to be eliminated. They have the technology to do it, but they don't have the management and governmental skills to face this cold reality.

This logic, however, is far from the minds of congressmen urging retaliation against Japan. Ask them why they are so upset about trade problems, and they will tell you they are concerned about people. Employment is the issue, not prices. Employment would have been a problem for the United States regardless of the Japanese. But it is much easier to attribute unemployment problems to Japanese imports.

If America were to become competitive in the international marketplace, reduction of labor content in whatever they do will be an unavoidable first step. This has nothing to do with imports. If American corporations wish to offer their customers a good value, year in, year out, they have to constantly remove labor content from their products so as not to pass on escalating wages.

This is what the Japanese manufacturers have been doing, because our customers do not accept inflationary pricing. Over time, this difference in the basic attitudes of Japanese and American manufacturers and consumers has resulted in a large difference in price competitiveness. Japanese competition has been a good thing for American and European consumers because they now have a choice.

Reflecting this, many Americans say they are against protectionism. Indeed, they unleash a flood of imports when they "vote" for Japanese products. But at election time in America, everyone agrees that the Japanese are villains and perpetrators of unemployment, casting their ballots for candidates who have enacted trade-limiting legislation, supposedly to create jobs.

Both Japanese and Americans increasingly act as if they see only one side of the issue at a time. Convenient momentary blindness enables them to appear consistent to themselves despite their contradictory behavior. Consumers put personal benefit ahead of national interest when they shop, but the state and its politicians whip up their nationalistic sentiment when they vote.

If only people were a little more aware of the realities of world trade, they might weigh fully both sides of the question. But they are not. Special interest groups and politicians in both Japan and the United States are exploiting the illusions of ordinary people in an attempt to justify waste and create unnatural tension. Despite our habit of waiting for consensus and wishing away conflict, we can't merely decry this situation. We need to take steps to expose these illusions. Our actions will be a start to solving complex but tractable problems. We can't afford protectionism, for we are not the mighty industrial giant we think we are.

THE MYTH OF JAPANESE MANAGEMENT

Despite our credo, which paints us as humble and starving, the Japanese are overconfident, even conceited, about the management ability of Japanese firms. There are few Japanese who are not convinced that our firms are far better managed than their foreign competitors. The praise continually lavished on Japanese-style management, à la Ezra Vogel, has made it difficult to believe the contrary.

But this complacency rests on a number of illusions. The first illusion is that the Japanese are hardworking by nature. Are we really exceptionally hard workers? Foreign production data on Honda, Sony, Matsushita, and other Japanese pioneers of multinationalization show little difference in productivity among workers in their plants in Japan, Europe, North America, and Asia.

There are, of course, differences but they result from factors such as subcontracting, vendors, and labor regulations. Once a plant begins regular production, productivity is more lastingly influenced by such factors as capital investment and management expertise, just as in Japan.

Observation of workers at Japanese municipal offices and the national railways dispels any illusions about the special diligence of the Japanese as a race. It is more logical to conclude that our industriousness is a response to necessity, and that when the Japanese are placed in situations that demand hard work, they work hard.

The youngest generation of job holders, products of affluent society, might even be innately lazy. They are products of parental indulgence and 16 years of uninspired education by teachers with no special fervor for their profession. Our supply of engineers and professional managers is surely endangered by this. And rather than running companies on the falsely comforting premise that the Japanese are industrious, it would be safer for us to recognize that the Japanese are very likely to abandon any pretense of diligence if not watched constantly. We ought to be worried and wary about what has happened to education and worker attitudes in the United States. It could happen in Japan, too—only faster. Our development has been accelerated, and so could our decline.

Outside experts on Japanese management also tell us that Japanese companies can rely on employee loyalty. It's not true. Not long ago I entered a barber shop on the basement floor of the Marunouchi Kokusai Building in the center of downtown Tokyo on a Saturday afternoon. I found the shop empty and was served immediately.

"Not many customers today, are there?" I said, relieved that I did not have to wait.

"That's right. Lately, business has been off Saturdays."

"When are you busiest?"

"Well, these days, around eleven, then around two or three in the afternoon on weekdays."

"But everyone around here must be working then. You mean during working hours?" I asked in disbelief.

"That's right. People these days don't want to spend their *own time* on things like haircuts."

"And in the past?"

"Well, a decade ago, we'd be busiest during the luncheon break and after five o'clock. Customers would rush to finish in less than 40 minutes."

On another occasion, I had a conversation with a taxicab driver. Because I was in a hurry, I asked for a receipt as soon as I got into the cab. The driver asked:

"Shall I just make it out for the meter fare?"

"What do you mean? Of course."

"Don't get me wrong, sir," he explained. "It's just that these days, people often tell me to write down double the fare, and offer to split the difference with me in exchange."

My conclusion from these and many other episodes is that our so-called company loyalty requires witnesses.

Other comparisons of our business practices and skills are possible. Many do not turn out in favor of the Japanese.

There are few phrases that express the essence of management as well as "a company is its people." But the majority of companies have been practicing the opposite of the Japanese management ethic. Today's view seems to be, "a company is its systems." And this approach is working. For a long time, we have assumed that our management system is the best system because we place so much importance on people. This, however, presumes that we work hard and think hard, given the opportunity. That was, on average, a good assumption when we were hungry, and when our companies were growing and giving promise to every employee. The situation today is fundamentally different. We are not worried about starvation. We *are* worried about our promotion because most of our companies have stopped growing. Many employees have become parasites of their company. "Office love" and "wining and dining" on the company are two of the new sports on the Japanese corporate scene.

The lesson now seems to be this: We *have* to tell employees exactly what we want from them. Americans are far ahead of us in this, as they have had to work with people who are less enthusiastic and gifted than our average employees. That's why they have developed a system using manuals, spelling out exactly what to do. In this way, they can make workers with modest education and intelligence perform well. Our system assumes that everyone has an IQ of 120. But that is no longer—indeed never was—the case. And that is precisely the reason why companies using, almost religiously, the American-style, manual-based approach are doing far better here than our traditionally managed companies.

Consider McDonald's, Mister Donut, 7-Eleven, and SECOM; each is at the top of its industry in Japan, and each, compared with its competitors, emphasizes (American-style) systems rather than (Japanese-style) people. Instead of hiring a small elite, they focus on dramatically improving the productivity of a large number of people with average qualifications. In short, they are applying pure American management systems.

The second- and third-best companies in their field may superficially appear to be using the same systems, but in fact continue to preach that "a company is its people." Unfortunately, this belief keeps them from using systems to best advantage. They begin to laud managers' "creative ingenuity" in actual work situations, and to make vague statements that only confuse the rank and file. Performance using such people-centered systems will vary considerably among territories and outlets because not every manager is creative and ingenious. Uniform excellence just cannot be counted on.

Inevitably, one must question two assumptions: (1) that each person possesses the intelligence and desire for achievement necessary to improve productivity through spontaneous creativity and ingenuity, and (2) that things do not have to be brought specifically to each person's attention.

It is true that an enterprise will succeed if it is staffed by the best people. But companies are lucky if they happen to find excellence in their managers; in general, bad managers are the majority. Can an enterprise assume that it is staffed by the best people available when it is forced to hire recent college graduates? A transition from Japanese- to American-style management has already become a general necessity in Japan, at least insofar as the younger generation of employees is concerned. The Americans are far ahead of us when it comes to working with a large number of less dedicated people. We need to recognize that Japan will need to turn to successful management formulas that permit both the bright few as well as the not-so-bright and energetic majority to get their job done with a minimum of confusion.

THE MYTH THAT TRADE IS OUR BIGGEST PROBLEM

Japan, like the rest of the advanced industrialized world, has many domestic industries that must be protected. Interestingly, we think we are the most open of trader nations and in the vanguard of free trade. Hence we accuse America of protectionism. Equally interesting, the Americans also think that they are in the vanguard of free trade, and accuse Japan of closing its markets. Both are wrong. As will become clear later, the Americans are already in Japan through direct operation, not through trading or exporting. The American people and government don't understand this because direct production and sales in Japan do not show up in American export figures.

On the other hand, the Japanese must never forget that we still have some areas of business protected by scores of regulations that disregard consumer interests, but that serve to protect Japanese rice and dairy farmers, retail banking, shops, trucking, oil refineries, health care and other service providers, and many other sectors. We are in no position to condemn the protectionism of others. Japan would clearly have much higher unemployment figures if we were forced by our trading partners to apply strict reciprocity and withdraw protection from domestic industries.

Our stonewalling on the trade issue has made us oblivious to other concerns of equal importance. When the United States criticized the weak yen, Japan moved to strengthen the dollar. The Japanese then heaved a collective sigh of relief in the innocent belief that this gesture of obedience would turn back the tide of protectionism in the United States by reducing the trade deficit. It won't, but more important, it will cause other problems for Japan.

Japan is now the world's largest creditor, and one of the most active. More than half of the dollars earned in Japan's trade with the world are recycled. For example, as much as $50 billion during 1985 went back to the United States, instead of being kept in Japan. This suggests that there are in fact few attractive opportunities to reinvest this money in Japan—itself a serious problem.

But there is another. Almost all of Japan's foreign assets are dollar-based. This means that if the value of its hard-earned dollars suddenly dwindles, the value of Japan's assets is reduced accordingly. Say that Japan's investment balance in the United States is worth $100 billion. If the value of the dollar falls by almost 10 percent in a short period (as it did in September–October of 1985), the loss will amount to $10 billion. Likewise, the interest return on investments in American financial institutions will be reduced by about 10 percent if converted back to yen.

Imports to Japan would increase by only about $6 billion if rice imports were completely liberalized. Assume that instead of making major unilateral concessions on the trade issue, Japan decided overnight to adopt a dollar-weakening policy that would have an equivalent impact. The resulting decrease in tax revenues due to lost profits by export-oriented firms would be worse than if it had taken the most sweeping possible market opening measures.

One of the most stringent protectionist bills, Texas Senator Lloyd Bentsen's proposal, calls for 25 percent across-the-board surcharge on "unfair" imports. One could argue that this ill-conceived bill would have been much better for Japan than the abrupt 50 percent appreciation of the yen over the past 12 months. The Bentsen bill would have affected all countries. But the strong yen affects only Japan, putting us at a considerable disadvantage compared with, say, a Newly Industrial Country (NIC), whose currency is generally pegged against the dollar.

Our perception gap here stems from an outdated view of Japan as a solely trade-dependent nation. Today Japan is also a creditor whose assets and claims must be protected. Nor should we forget that Japan is a huge market for consumer goods and a buyer of foreign goods and services. The Japanese should realize that they are the biggest customer in the world for American farmers and multinationals and convert this fact into political clout, should the need arise. Trade is only one of many activities we conduct today. We simply give too much importance to it, and lose big in the final analysis.

WE CAN BE TEACHERS

The Japanese are more than just world traders. We should realize that having raised our per capita GNP from a few hundred dollars to more than $10,000 in less than 40 years, we have valuable experience in the field of economic development. Japan is probably the only instructor qualified to teach countries on the road to industrialization how to draft and implement specific economic and educational policies.

Japan also has a great number of low-paid, college-trained engineers. This makes it a potential supplier of the conscientious engineering talent that the world so sorely needs.

Japan could assist Brazil and other debt-ridden countries—and contribute to international amity in the process—by buying land using money from its huge purse full of dollars, money that is of no use whatsoever unless invested or spent productively. The indebted Latin American countries have land, but no money. Japan has money, but no land. It was not so long ago that the United States bought Louisiana from France and Alaska from Russia. The idea of large-scale land purchases should therefore not be brushed off without consideration. We don't have to own the land, but we would need to ensure free access in order for our security-conscious food protectionists to feel relaxed about growing rice and other agricultural products on foreign soil, be it purchased or leased. In other words, we have to realize that even land could be "imported" to solve the most difficult problem nature has given us, our small island. Money can solve the problem, so long as we have the mental flexibility to search for unconventional solutions.

It is important and timely for us to rethink our preconceptions about Japan. What is Japan? What can it do? Japan's tragic decision to build a strong army for a rich nation 120 years ago after the Meiji Restoration, and its reliance on manufacturing trade after World War II, both focused too narrowly on only one aspect of Japan. It's time to think about the whole picture. With the money and people we now possess, we can do it.

Companies without Countries

When agricultural production and primary commodities were local by nature and constituted the bulk of countries' exports, trade balances were a reasonably accurate measure of respective economic strength. Mines and farms were on the country's team and whoever exported the most was the winner. But no longer. Today, the flow of goods across national borders is of much less relevance. Lines on a map mean little to a corporation. When a firm is considering where to build a plant, it bases its decisions for the most part on the economic merits of the location, wherever it may be. And it is more likely to break up production, making several components in several locations, or farm out the production of some components to foreign suppliers.

Trade is just one of several options a corporation can choose in order to create wealth. For example, a company may find a joint venture partner or acquire one, build an offshore plant, or license a foreign company to produce its products and services. In all these cases, there will be no traffic of goods across the ocean, hence no trade will take place. A corporation is interested in the bottom-line results, not in helping government cash registers ring at the port of export.

Despite these changes, our way of keeping score, and the politicians and bureaucrats who keep score, haven't changed.

Say, for example, that an American firm in Cleveland closes an unprofitable plant and moves to California. If the plant subsequently fails in California, the firm might then move it to Japan. As soon as it moves to Japan, the goods it used to export to Japan when it was located in Ohio and California disappear from the trade statistics. Although the firm is still an American company, its products are no longer counted as American exports to users back in the United States. Their sale now counts in the trade statistics as *Japanese* exports to the United States. In the minds of policy makers this means lost jobs and profits. Who is to blame?

Wholly U.S.-owned Texas Instruments in Japan exported about half of its sales ($567 million) in fiscal 1984, and most went to the United States, albeit via Singapore for final assembly. These sales were a significant factor in the recent growth both in Japan's exports and in U.S. high-tech imports.

A number of American firms have moved to Taiwan, but Taiwan has few indigenous products to offer to the United States. Low-cost goods made in Taiwan in plants built by American firms, or made by small Taiwanese-owned plants on order from American firms, are sent to the United States and appear on the trade statistics as a flood of Taiwanese exports.

Reading the old trade scorecard, the American government has reacted to this "Taiwanese" export surplus, which now amounts to $13 billion a year, by demanding that Taiwan open its market and buy goods from the United States. This, despite the fact that it was the Americans who created this "export" problem. Taiwan can't balance trade with the United States. Relatively poor Taiwanese, at $2,000 per capita GNP, would have to spend one third of their personal income on U.S. goods to rectify the U.S.-Taiwan trade imbalance.

The world economy is now ruled by manufacturing and trading corporations, not nations. Corporations move into new areas before anything else; nations follow, trying to measure progress with antiquated statistical instruments. Nevertheless, we continue to talk about trade friction based on balances that in no way reflect total corporate activities. To really understand the state of the world economy, a broader concept of trade is necessary. It is important to find what American and Japanese companies are really doing in each others' country. When we do, the results are surprising.

THERE IS NO IMBALANCE BETWEEN THE
UNITED STATES AND JAPAN

Like other images and accusations we have accepted, the American view that trade between the United States and Japan is unbalanced has also come to be taken for granted in Japan. We worry that the Americans are angry at our "export surplus." The way they see it, the flow of goods is a one-way flood into the United States, robbing Americans of jobs. Meanwhile, they say, Japan tries to prevent American products from entering, and non-tariff barriers compound the difficulties.

The Japanese Ministry of Foreign Affairs usually tries to cool American tempers by promising further market liberalization. Officially, Japan tries to meet the other side halfway. But does a U.S.-Japan trade imbalance really exist in the first place? Why have we accepted this "fact"—especially since it isn't true? Our markets may be protected in some cases (e.g., rice, financial services), but we are buying a large amount of American goods. These purchases are hidden, however, because goods manufactured by American companies in Japan and shipped to the United States count as Japanese exports to the United States, whereas those sold to users in Japan by the same U.S. companies count as neither exports nor imports and do not show up on the trade statistics on either side.

In 1984, production and sales by American companies in Japan—counting only the 300 largest manufacturing firms out of roughly 3,000 in Japan—totaled $43.9 billion.[1] IBM-Japan, Texas Instruments Japan, NCR, Fuji Xerox, Coca-Cola, Yokogawa-Hewlett-Packard, AMP, and Molex are all examples of how American companies are doing a booming business in Japan. In contrast, direct production by Japanese companies in the United States, which has picked up speed with the entry of automobile manufacturers in the past few years, still totaled only $12.8 billion in fiscal 1984.

Leaving aside for a moment the comparison of data on goods crossing U.S. and Japanese borders (customs statistics), let us turn to real trade, that is, the measure of how much people in

---

[1]In 1985, it exceeded $51 billion, a figure greater than the American trade deficit of $49.7 billion with Japan. (Source: U.S. Customs/McKinsey analysis.)

FIGURE 1   Presence of Americans and Japanese in Each Other's Marketplace (1984)

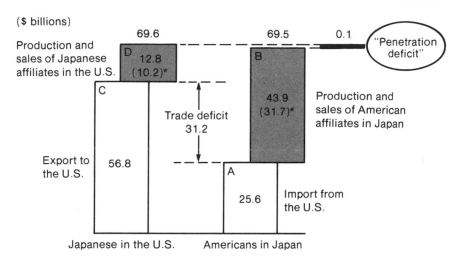

($ billions)

*Portion represented by actual equity position: Americans in Japan = 72.2%
Japanese in the U.S. = 80.0%

SOURCE: McKinsey & Company, Inc.

each country are paying for goods manufactured by companies from other countries (Figure 1).

Japan imports goods worth $25.6 billion *A* and buys made-in-Japan American goods worth $43.9 billion *B* a year. The sum of these two figures could be considered an index of "product presence." In total, American companies have $69.5 billion worth of product presence in Japan.[2]

Correspondingly, the United States imports $56.8 billion worth of goods *C* from Japan and buys $12.8 billion worth of goods *D* manufactured and sold in the United States by Japanese firms.

---

[2]This may still underestimate America's product presence in Japan. In a book based on a McKinsey study for the U.S.–Japan Trade Study Group (*Japan: Obstacles and Opportunities*, New York: John Wiley & Sons, 1983), I argued that Americans could have sold another $60 billion of goods in Japan had they not chosen instead to license production to Japanese companies (for which they received $800 million per year in fees).

The total is $69.9 billion, almost the same as the figure for Japan. In other words, the product presence, or market penetration, of both countries into each other's turf is now practically identical.

The irony is that when patent licenses and royalties are added to the balance, the balance shifts heavily in favor of the United States, which exports to Japan far more technology (in, for example, nuclear power, aviation, space and drugs) and licenses far more franchises (e.g., Denny's, 7-Eleven, Mister Donut)—not to mention computer software—than Japan does to the United States.

Now then, why is it that the Americans are upset by Japanese trade practices? There are two broad reasons. The first is that most Americans do not know how successful American corporations have become "insiders" in Japan. They read too much about how the government schemes to make Japanese markets closed or difficult to enter. The Japanese government probably has the worst public relations capabilities of all major countries. They cannot even communicate a simple fact. Thus, we are leaving the entire information supply on the trade issue to the American side. Silence is golden, we say. But in this day and age of mass media, we have to learn to speak up.

The second reason is that the Americans want jobs, not a trade balance. But they don't say it that way, because they feel a little embarrassed to say, "Give us jobs." So when they talk to the Japanese, they say "open your markets," implying that Japanese markets are closed. If they were closed, why would American companies produce (and sell) as much as $44 billion dollars (or $51 billion in 1985) in Japan? Many critics of Japan argue that the jobs Americans lost to the Japanese are the sum of B and C in Figure 1. Jobs corresponding to the sum of A and D are created in the United States. Hence there is an imbalance of jobs, they argue, equivalent to some $62 billion.[3] We sit in Japan and listen to the Americans demand that the Japanese change regu-

---

[3]The validity of this argument is questionable. Herbert Stein pointed out in a recent *Wall Street Journal* editorial (July 29, 1986) that the United States has created several million new jobs at the same time that its trade balance was shifting from positive to negative. He argues that foreign investment of dollars obtained through trade has helped to create these new jobs in the United States.

lations, import procedures, exchange rates, interest rates, and even our "culture" of savings. We have done most of these things. But we did nothing to create jobs in America. Let's face it. We cannot solve our problems unless we understand what the Americans really want. If it's jobs, then we have to answer in one of several ways. First, we can ask the American corporations in Japan to go home. Since we will still buy American products, if they are distributed and priced the same as today, there will be an increase of $44 billion (corresponding to B in Figure 1) of American exports to Japan. Would American multinationals do this? I doubt it. But, our request would at least make it clear that the trade imbalance is largely caused by American multinationals' individual corporate decisions, not by the unfair practices of the Japanese.

Or, we should ask Japanese multinationals to go to the United States and produce, rather than exporting out of Japan. This would reveal how difficult it is for Japanese corporations to manufacture their products in the United States, and would help strip away many myths about the excellence of Japanese management. On an equal footing with the Americans, that is, working with the American labor vendors, the Japanese are no better, no worse, than Americans in managing a sizable company. Our trade record shows that differences in culture and language make it a handicap for us to produce in the United States. These are the industries Americans themselves have given up at home. Why should the Japanese succeed using the same labor force and wage rate?

Despite this track record of failures, there are "warning signs" reported in the United States that the Japanese are taking over industries, banks, and real estate. Thus, when the United States demands that Japan help create jobs in the United States, we have to make sure that we are *invited* to do so. If we enter American turf at random, it will only enhance anti-Japanese feelings.

In at least one sense, then, the trade imbalance is fictitious. The information about real trade provided in Figure 1 rather than customs statistics shows that (1) American firms are doing very well in Japan, (2) the Japanese are buying a great deal of American goods, and (3) U.S.-Japanese relations in substantive terms are much better than most people realize. But if the United States wants jobs, it will have to say so to the Japanese so that we can come up with a concrete set of action plans rather than unclear accusations.

WHY SPENDING ANOTHER $100 ON IMPORTS WON'T DO ANY GOOD

If we calculate per capita spending on goods made by U.S. companies and partners, we find that each Japanese on average spends $583 a year on American goods, and each American $298 on Japanese goods (Figure 2). The data in these figures were adjusted to account for the fact that American joint ventures in Japan are usually not 100 percent American owned. The percentage of Japanese ownership and production was subtracted from total production in Japan to reflect the degree of actual foreign participation in manufacturing. Thus, 50 percent of Fuji Xerox's annual sales of $1.7 billion is attributable to Rank-Xerox, the U.S.-U.K. joint venture, and the remaining 50 percent to Fuji Film. When the data are adjusted in this way, it becomes apparent that the Japanese are spending about twice as much per capita on American goods as vice versa. The reason, of course, is that Japan's population of about 120 million is less than half that of the United States. Despite the population differential, the Japanese are managing to support equal product presence. In order to "balance" the trade, an average Japanese must spend twice as much on American goods as the average American does on Japanese goods.

Spending as a percentage of income is another interesting way to look at the statistics. The average Japanese spends about 6 percent of his income on American products, but the average American only 2 percent of his. It is not surprising that most Japanese balked at Prime Minister Nakasone's appeals to spend another $100 on imports. They are already buying U.S. products, and there aren't many areas where they could possibly spend more. The foreign goods the Japanese really want to buy are available already. Schick, Del Monte, Coca-Cola, IBM, and many others who came to Japan long ago are now well established and successful. If The Coca-Cola Company were not already in Japan, the Japanese would be happy to buy an extra $100 worth of its products. But the products with enough appeal to cross the Pa-

FIGURE 2   Value of Consumer Purchases (1984, Dollars per Capita)

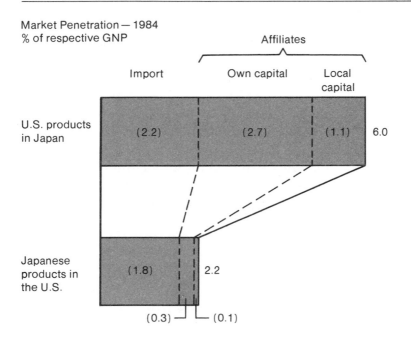

Market Penetration — 1984
% of respective GNP

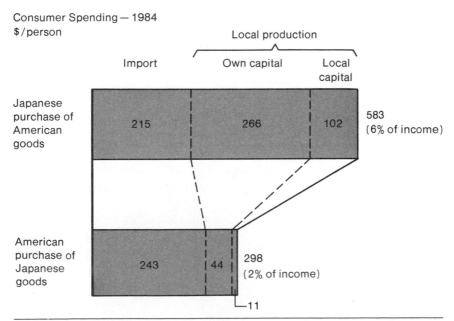

SOURCE: McKinsey & Company, Inc.

cific are already present in the Japanese market. The rest—the metal bats, plywood, cigarettes, and so on—often create heated discussions between the United States and Japan, but are peanuts, not worth making an issue of. Import restrictions on these goods have triggered more concern than their potential sales should warrant.

Most articles about trade do not distinguish between export and direct overseas production. American companies are all over Europe and they are strong. Both GM and Ford each have over a 10 percent share of the pan-European automobile market. Nissan and Toyota have only 2.8 and 2.6 percent, respectively. Americans are really dominant and well accepted in Europe. The problem is that none of their cars are exported out of the United States. This leads Japanese (and American) managers to wrongly assume that American companies are losing international competitiveness because their exports are dwindling. On the contrary, in almost every key market of the world, American companies are becoming formidable insiders particularly their service industries, such as banks, rent-a-cars, hotels, and charge cards. And this trend has intensified over the past 10 years.

EURO–AMERICAN CORPORATIONS IN JAPAN

How have foreign firms succeeded in Japan, an unforgivingly competitive marketplace where every year 19,000 of its indigenous firms go bankrupt? There are not any formulas for success, but many good examples.[4]

Wella, the German hair care company, avoided direct competition with Japan's giant and well-established makers, whose shampoos lined the same supermarket shelves with soaps and toothpastes. Wella initially decided to sell its shampoos as hair care products, using barber shops and beauty parlors as channels, and later as beauty aids, using the same distribution channels as cosmetics and luxury beauty products.

Wella's first Japanese president Dr. Dieter K. Schneidewind's account of his difficulties in getting his product accepted in Japan is an entertaining story of entrepreneurship. For example, he paid

---

[4]Actually, there are some generalizations one can make, as I did in *Obstacles and Opportunities* (New York: John Wiley & Sons, 1983), pp. 102–5.

daily visits to high-class bar madams on the Ginza to promote his products. To get Japan Airlines stewardesses to use Wella products (remember, in those days, the JAL stewardesses were from good families), he met with the vice president of the stewardesses' union—and later married her. Thanks to these pioneering efforts, Wella products began to be sold in drug stores, at cosmetics counters in department stores, in beauty parlors, at hair dressers, and through a score of distribution channels previously unheard of in Japan. Today, Wella products are sold everywhere, even in supermarkets with the standard brands, but the way Schneidewind initially placed them in prestigious environments gave them a high-quality image that they have retained. In the process of penetrating Japan, Wella developed a formula for the "hard" hair of the Japanese. The R&D knowledge is now applied in products for American blacks and Asian consumers.

Warner-Lambert joined forces with Seiko to sell Schick razors through a nationwide network of specialized cutlery wholesalers. It revolutionized the early-morning habits of Japanese men when it introduced shaving cream and disposable blades. Before, Japanese men had shaved at night when they took their bath after coming home, but Schick's ingenious campaign made shaving a morning performance.

In a little more than 10 years after forming his 50-50 joint venture with McDonald's, Den Fujita has risen to the top of the fast-food industry in Japan. Today, 550 McDonald's stores scattered across Japan gross nearly $770 million yearly. McDonald's succeeded in the United States by expanding its chains in the suburbs, but Fujita concentrated initially on downtown Tokyo and other major urban districts. He was smart not to follow the American pattern.

To be first into the market is usually a requirement for success in Japan, because the Japanese tend to view the first entry as the "original" product. Coca-Cola began lining up bottler-distributorships before restrictions on foreign capital were lifted. Its competitors waited until the change had been made and arrived a year afterwards. This difference continues to have an effect even today, 30 years later. Coca-Cola now enjoys a lead that no one, not even Japanese makers, can contest. It controls 60 percent of the entire soft drink market in Japan. Coca-Cola's contribution to Japan has been to challenge our time-honored wholesaler-retailer distribution methods with its unique, "direct route" sales force.

Its early arrival is not, of course, the only reason for Coca-Cola's success. In Japan, where vending machines are the main distribution channel, the company would not have been able to maintain its share with Coca-Cola alone, because most vending machines have more than eight selections. To keep its enemies at bay, it developed and marketed allied products such as Hi-C (fruit juices), Georgia Coffee (canned coffee), Real Gold (a vitamin drink), and Aquarius (a sport drink), which it does not handle in the United States. Coke is now the largest distributor of canned coffee in Japan. A wholly dependent subsidiary tied down by directives from American headquarters would not have been able to do this.

Being first into Japan's market does not, however, guarantee success. Dunkin' Donuts joined forces with the big Seibu restaurant chain before any other American doughnut chain came to Japan. Its first store was opened on a corner of the Ginza amidst high-class shops and department stores. Mister Donut arrived later and tied up with Duskin (then practically unknown, now a leading manufacturer and distributor of mops and cleaning cloths).

Koji Chiba at Mister Donut realized that his firm could not compete with Dunkin' Donuts on an equal footing. He therefore set up a model shop in Mino, an undistinguished suburb of Osaka, to show prospective franchises that a Mister Donut store could survive even in a bad location. Potential franchisees, visiting the Mino shop, realized without being told that their own sites were comparable or superior, and therefore had good chances of success. Franchises spread rapidly. Dunkin' Donuts has only 65 shops despite strenuous efforts to expand, while the latecomer Mister Donut has 415 with over $300 million annual turnover. Mister Donut's success was due to Chiba's having seen through and remedied a flaw in his opponent's strategy: Few small businessmen were willing to put themselves in the same class as a Ginza location.

Reports *The New York Times:*

> Market analysts here cite Mister Donut as a first-class example of a fairly common phenomenon: a lower-ranked American com-

pany that outperforms its top-ranked American competition in Japan. This is a country where Schick outsells Gillette and Del Monte ketchup is more popular than Heinz.[5]

EVOLUTION OF A MULTINATIONAL CORPORATION

To better understand the forces behind the trade deficit, it's important to understand how a corporation becomes a multinational, and how that process affects the trade imbalance. In McKinsey, we use a concept called a business system. It is a mnemonic for breaking down a company's operations into its major functions and activities—basically R&D, manufacturing, sales, and service (Figure 3).

The parts of this business system move offshore predictably as a multinational company grows. Era I of this process (Figure 4) is the export phase. Most Japanese companies passed through this era during the 1960s. They used trading companies to export their goods across the ocean, and relied heavily on an often exclusive local distributor.

This became a problem when the company wanted to do sophisticated marketing in order to get better access to customers. Thus, they moved into Era II, establishing their own subsidiaries with marketing, sales, and service functions. Most Japanese corporations are in that phase today.

Some companies, such as Honda and Nissan, have moved their production, at least partially, to the United States and Europe. Likewise, many Americans have aggressively moved into Era III, as production at home has become prohibitively expensive or difficult. However, most corporations in Era III do not integrate their local production and sales into one unit. For example, Nissan's plant in Tennessee reports into the headquarter's production function, while their U.S. sales company in California reports into the Overseas Business department in Tokyo. This format usually enables the local operations to enhance functional competences, but does not allow it to act as an integrated organization, responsible for price, cost, and volume—three key elements that determine profit.

---

[5]Terry Trucco, "Serving Mister Donut and the Community," *The New York Times*, December 26, 1982, p. 6.

FIGURE 3 The Business System

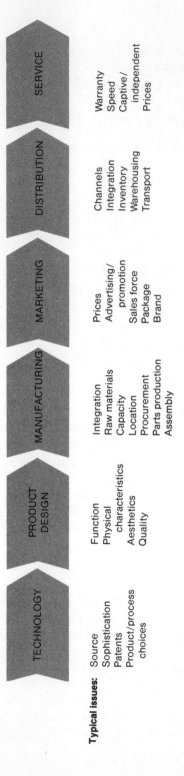

TECHNOLOGY	PRODUCT DESIGN	MANUFACTURING	MARKETING	DISTRIBUTION	SERVICE
Typical issues: Source Sophistication Patents Product/process choices	Function Physical characteristics Aesthetics Quality	Integration Raw materials Capacity Location Procurement Parts production Assembly	Prices Advertising/promotion Sales force Package Brand	Channels Integration Inventory Warehousing Transport	Warranty Speed Captive/independent Prices

SOURCE: McKinsey & Company, Inc.

FIGURE 4 Evolution of a Multinational

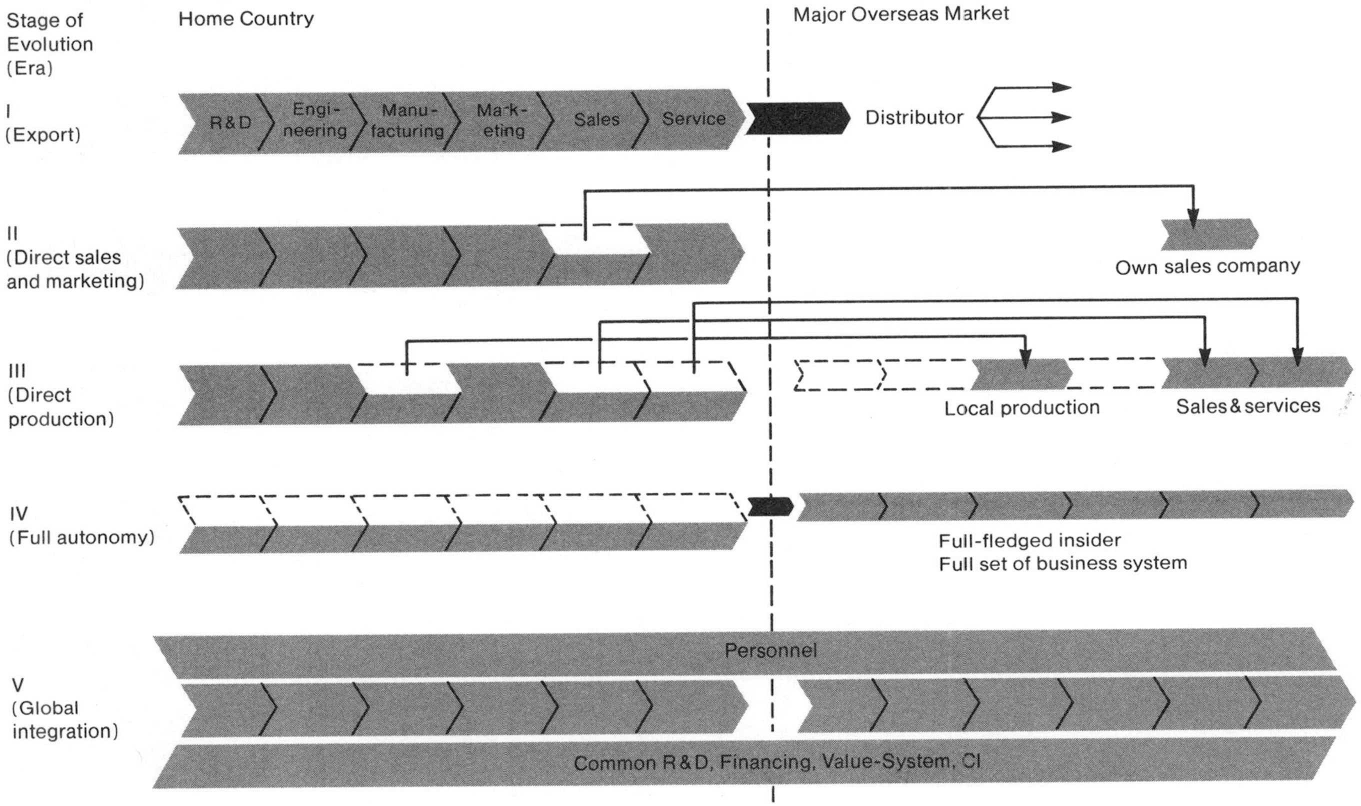

Stage of Evolution (Era)	Home Country					Major Overseas Market
	R&D	Engi-neering	Manu-facturing	Ma-rk-eting	Sales	Service

I (Export) — Distributor

II (Direct sales and marketing) — Own sales company

III (Direct production) — Local production / Sales & services

IV (Full autonomy) — Full-fledged insider / Full set of business system

V (Global integration) — Personnel / Common R&D, Financing, Value-System, CI

SOURCE: McKinsey & Company, Inc.

If the company wants to become a full-fledged insider, it needs to transfer such functions as R&D, engineering, and financing—Era IV in Figure 4. At this stage, the local company has all of the minimum necessary functions to compete effectively against local incumbents on an equal footing and can respond to local customer needs.

IBM recently moved into this phase by transferring the part of its headquarters responsible for the Asia-Pacific region from Mt. Pleasant (New York) to Tokyo. It is totally responsible for such dynamic and competitive markets as Japan, Korea, China, Australia, and the Association of Southeast Asian Nations (ASEAN). Before this move, IBM-Japan already had a basic research laboratory, local product development laboratories, and other key functions in Japan.

While some Japanese corporations have established R&D facilities in Europe and the United States, for example, Otsuka Pharmaceutical, no one has truly moved into Era IV. This lag in development in the evolution makes Japanese companies dependent on exports while the most developed American companies are disappearing from Uncle Sam's trade statistics as they move far into Era III and to some extent even to Era IV.

Although no company has done so, these vanguard multinationals need yet to move into a fifth and final phase of the evolution, that is, a stage called global integration. Era IV companies are autonomous and dynamic. However, they do not behave like one truly multinational and global operator. For example, most companies in Eras III and IV leave the hiring and development of managers to their local management. This makes it unlikely that a person hired by a subsidiary will ever find his or her way to the top of the parent corporation. In Japan we have double standards even for the Japanese. Those who are hired in April by the "legitimate" recruiting process fresh out of college get the right-of-way over employees with previous job experience who consequently join the company in other months besides April. Not surprisingly, then, headquarters personnel departments often do not even have files on foreign local managers. Japanese corporations are not alone in their parochialism. The top management of a German company is almost always German, a Swiss company's is Swiss, and an American multinational's headquarters is basically American. McKinsey is probably one of the very few corporations whose senior management (our Executive and Shareholders committees), consists of nationals from countries where we have substantial consulting practices. The United States, Britain, Japan, Holland, Germany, and other countries are represented on these managing committees.

In this final phase of globalization, companies realize that it is much cheaper and cleverer to conduct basic and common R&D throughout the world and finance its cash requirements worldwide. Its key managers, whatever their origin, share a strong corporate identity. Frequent exchange of people, face-to-face meetings, and product swapping among its full-fledged subsidiaries are characteristic of corporations in Era V. The corporations are both local and global. Employees identify more strongly with the corporation than with the nation in which they operate. They can relate the local customers with the customers in other parts of the world and vice versa. Some European and American corporations are now searching for ways to move into Era V, in order to attract and keep the best possible personnel, regardless of nationality, religion, and gender. Japanese companies are far behind this and don't even begin to understand the requirements, particularly in personnel, to succeed in the key markets of the world.

JAPANESE CORPORATIONS LACK INTERNATIONAL MANAGEMENT SAVVY

The Japanese tend to think that the U.S.-Japan "trade imbalance" is caused by Japanese industry's greater relative competitiveness. Thus, one myth leads to another. But as we have seen, the real cause of the apparent imbalance is local production and sales by American companies in Japan.

Looking at it another way, Japanese corporations have to resort to exports because their methods have generally not yet evolved sufficiently to accommodate local production, in the United States and Europe especially. Those with the real management and production know-how cross the Pacific and manufacture close to their market, like the Americans. Once local plants are built, products stay in the country where they are produced.

The question for a Japanese business strategist to ask is: How well developed is the ability of Japanese firms to produce locally? And how can it be improved? In 1984, Japanese firms produced only $14 billion worth of goods in the United States, compared to the $44 billion produced by American firms in Japan. Except for a few cases of successful production in the United States by outstanding Japanese companies—Yoshida Kogyo Kabushiki-gaisha (YKK, the fastener maker), Honda, Sony, Kikkoman, Nissan, Matsushita, and a few others—the majority are barely afloat and hardly one has been able to increase its profits steadily. Most pay for themselves only when business is good, and flounder when it's bad. Their management isn't any more stable; the top local managers are replaced every few years with new men from Japan, the locally hired American managers don't try to make themselves understood to Japanese headquarters, and indecisiveness about directions is the order of the day—every day.

For a firm to go international takes not years but decades, and success depends on a long-term perspective. The founder or his counterpart must be able to command respect and trust. He must be able to say, "I want you to go" to his overseas representative, who will have to commit 10 to 20 years of his life to the task. Results will not be seen in less time.

The person in charge overseas must realize that to establish oneself requires the same effort as to found and establish a new firm, and that without enduring effort, success will never be achieved. Sony's current chairman, Akio Morita, made that kind of effort as Sony's first president in the United States, crossing the Pacific over 300 times to ensure that its overseas operations succeeded.

In most Japanese firms, a manager may spend up to 10 years overseas only to find himself at the bottom of the career escalator when he comes back to Japan. In Japan, any opinion that smacks of having adapted well to life abroad invites rejection. Like Americans who frequently distrust veteran expatriates, the Japanese are wary of returnees. This intolerance obviously does nothing to foster internationally minded initiative and leadership.

The only sectors that are still trying to expand their overseas operations with the organization-man approach are trading companies and banks. Manufacturers, unless they are managed by strong personalities, have virtually never achieved success with this approach. Overseas operations just cannot be built up with people from headquarters doing two- to four-year stints abroad.

American firms in Japan are much better placed. IBM is in a class by itself, with 18,000 employees, yearly sales of $6 billion, and ordinary profit approaching $1 billion, and more engineering graduates vying to enter it each year than any other corporation in Japan. But many other American companies in Japan have enviable market shares and income. As mentioned earlier, Coca-Cola not only has 60 percent of the Japanese soft drink market, but also holds first place in canned coffee (Georgia Coffee) sold from vending machines. Schick, Gillette, Vicks, Contac, and Johnson & Johnson are all familiar brands, while NCR, Yokogawa-Hewlett-Packard, AMP, Texas Instruments, and Molex are all strong office equipment and capital goods manufacturers. If you add to the list of successful American manufacturers in Japan such names as Baskin-Robbins, Haagen-Dazs and Hobsons, you'd wonder why Americans are so self-critical about their success abroad. By contrast, the Japanese are in deep trouble in really getting into key market places such as the United States and Europe. Our success has been limited to exporting our products as a foreigner, but not as an insider.

American firms are generally strong everywhere overseas, not just in Japan. They have large market shares in many sectors in Europe. Even some that have not done so well in Japan—like the semiconductor maker Intel, Ford, General Motors, and Kodak—are virtual insiders in the European market. In credit cards, hotels, banks, car rentals, and other services, American firms carry out international operations on a far greater scale than the Japanese.

The management ability of American firms has been proven on a global scale. America's current deindustrialization and the general weakening of its international position are not attributable to a weakening of American management, the way many of us in Japan like to think. And the recent strength of Japan's industrial base is not attributable to the improved international management ability of the Japanese. On the contrary, lulled into complacency by enviably pacific labor relations and superbly responsive suppliers, the international management of Japanese companies has in general grown weaker, not stronger, despite the trade figures. Japanese products find buyers abroad, but Japanese direct investments and acquisitions continue to fail.

Foreign praise of Japanese management must not be taken at face value. It is directed at the management methods of a minority of Japanese firms manufacturing primarily in Japan. Paradoxically, the U.S.-Japan trade "imbalance" might even be attributed to the gap between inept international management by Japanese firms and the multinational skills of American firms.

In order for Japanese firms to multinationalize to the same extent as American and Swiss corporations, they will need to retrain staff, reform head office organizations, draft written work procedures (manuals are neglected in Japan), accept personnel with foreign backgrounds in their directorates, conform accounting and financing procedures to international practices, improve the career paths open to locally hired management, and address a dizzying list of other areas where they have yet to internationalize. The message is simple: Japanese firms cannot afford to rest on their laurels.

Opening Communications as Well as Markets

Like a clumsy, unarmed giant, Japan stumbles through storms without making the slightest effort to find shelter or protection. Not surprisingly, it gets savage treatment from every quarter. It is time that Japan learned to communicate in ways that enable the world to understand it better. The tidal wave of internationalization has made it necessary to express fine shades of meaning and feeling.

Misunderstandings about Japan are the natural outcome of mistaken Japanese perceptions about the world. Very few people in Japan have made any effort to make themselves or their country understood. We continue to think that if we shake our heads long enough and complain softly, eventually the world will understand us. We don't understand that today's global society is radically different from consensual Japan. People don't usually come to a tacit understanding without pressure being exerted visibly.

We don't realize that when someone has something to communicate to someone from another culture, he or she must organize the facts and try to persuade the listener in a logical way—that it is necessary to be prepared to counter new and unforeseen criticisms aggressively.

Nor do we realize that global economics are such that simple confrontations, with a winner and a loser, have been replaced by more complex situations where ties must be the objective and cooperation the primary tactic. We must learn to act and communicate so that our market conquests do not become Pyrrhic victories.

WE ARE AMERICA'S BIGGEST CUSTOMER

The debate about our agriculture market is a good example of how we (1) don't know the facts and (2) thus fail to communicate/ challenge inaccurate accusations. Most American critics of Japan describe our market as closed. They tell us to buy beef and oranges with a tone that implies that we don't even know what beef and oranges taste like.

The fact is that the Japanese buy more agricultural commodities from the United States than any other country. In 1984, we imported 71 percent of the beef and veal, 29 percent of the oranges, and 56 percent of the grapefruit exported by the United States. That same year, our imports of corn, soy beans, wheat, and other products ranked above every other country's. Japan paid $6.756 billion for American agricultural produce, far ahead of the runners-up USSR at $2.8 billion and the Netherlands at $2.3 billion. Japan should be described as a Class A customer for American produce—already.

That does not prove that our markets are entirely open. They are not. But every country in the world defends its farmers. American farmers, too, are protected from the Australians and Argentinians by tariffs. Nevertheless, with the exception of rice, the list of our import statistics clearly demonstrates the openness of Japan's agricultural markets—or our inability to grow some crops. The Americans have little reason to upbraid their best customer. If anything, they should be ashamed of not realizing this. It is not a question of the Japanese market being closed, but one of *increasing* already considerable purchases. For months, we have been holding "market-opening" talks as if we were about to begin buying our first-ever side of beef. This has created the false impression that transactions are about to start from zero. The correct term is *market expansion*. And the sooner we begin using it, the sooner both Americans and Japanese will recognize reality in this sector of our bilateral trade.

But that is our problem. We don't communicate. Nor do we get the facts necessary to substantiate or refute what other nations claim about Japan. We accept the accusations and images thrust upon us and silently hope the world's anger will subside.

In the brief space of 40 years, the Japanese government has reduced the agricultural population from 35 percent to 6 percent, and is working on reducing farm acreage. If we explained to foreigners that this reduction could not have been achieved without tremendous efforts to overcome conflicts with farmers, at least a few of them would be forced to acknowledge that the Japanese government has pursued an open agricultural policy.

SEGMENTING THE POLITICAL MARKET

We also assume that all Americans, our chief disparagers, speak with one voice. Every voice is the voice of MacArthur and every critic the voice of America. This is not true. America, like Japan, has special interests. We need to identify those groups, particularly those whose interests coincide with ours.

For example, Japan is now the biggest buyer of American beef in the world. If Japan did exactly as "America" demands and completely liberalized its market, Japan would buy *less* American beef, because cheaper Australian beef would flood the market. Japan's present quota system currently protects weaker American producers.

Or, if Japan bought more beef *it would buy five times less corn and feed grains.* If Japan agreed to buy more beef, the result would be the collapse of the Japanese livestock industry, which up to now has purchased American corn and feed grains as cattlefeed. With every additional ton of beef imported, corn imports would be reduced by five tons.

We need to point out more articulately that the interests of American livestockers and corn farmers are opposed.

The same argument can be used with those who complain that Japanese cigarette manufacturers are not letting foreign cigarettes into the Japanese market. Japan buys $1.5 billion of American tobacco leaves annually. If Japan completely deregulated imports of foreign cigarettes, fewer cigarettes would be sold by Japanese manufacturers because the market is unlikely to grow. Smoking in Japan, like in the United States, is a declining habit. This means imports of American tobacco leaves would decrease correspondingly. American tobacco farmers would come out losers. Not only would they sell less tobacco, they would sell it at lowered prices. In the United States, the big tobacco companies are so powerful that they can buy tobacco at prices less attractive to growers than what the Japanese Tobacco Corporation will pay.

SPECIAL INTERESTS VERSUS THE COMMON INTEREST

So the forces behind "American" pressure on Japan are quite different from what the Japanese conceive them to be. Special interest groups speak in America's name, but they are not America. There is no one American public. Different groups within the U.S. government and in different states hold differing views.

Why is it, then, that when one of these groups speaks up, Japan begins to excuse itself as if it had a guilty conscience? There is no reason for Japan to quake and tremble every time a lobby in Washington makes the newspaper headlines. We should be responsive, but it is more important for us to make a greater effort to find out exactly what is at stake, who stands to benefit, and who stands to lose when a lobby calls for Japan to open a market.

Pressure can be met by counterpressure. When the livestock farmers complain, Japanese corn buyers should approach the American corn and grain growers' associations with a simple message: "Look, if we go out of business, you're going to suffer, too. We're in this together." If American corn and feed grain growers realized what is at stake, they would be more likely to exert pressure on the cattle farmers to be content with their current export levels or at least compete with them in Washington for political favors. The cigarette issue could also be dealt with in the same way.

We should not try to manipulate American public opinion. What we should do is try to inform relevant and economically friendly parts of it. But we don't. Our communications and public relations are nonexistent or at best naive. When a textile bill by Congressman Edward Jenkins is being debated in Washington, you can be sure that Singaporean Prime Minister Lee Kwan Yew will be there to protect his country's interests. But when an issue arises involving the Japanese we call our lobbyists. More important, we don't communicate with audiences that will be directly concerned. The result is that those who should be lending a hand in their own interest stand idly by as opponents of Japan make most of the news headlines.

It is close to impossible for the interests of every citizen of a nation to coincide on even a single issue. To say that the United States is opposed to Japanese car imports is simplistic. Imported car dealers obviously want to import as many cars as possible, and many drivers want to buy Japanese cars.

Japan's leaders, most of whom are one generation older than mine, were so emotionally scarred by Japan's defeat in World War II and by the occupation that they still tend to see everything in terms of the vanquished having to do what the victors command. They still think in terms of the "winner" taking all, as if discussions on complex issues could be this clear-cut. So they avoid discussion.

We must learn how to reach small groups of people and try to convince them as individuals. "America" doesn't listen or think, but Americans do. And when I say we, I don't mean the Japanese government. "We" are no more a monolith than the United States. Each of us, companies and individuals, has a responsibility to communicate our position to the United States. Even if different Japanese voices end up in conflict with each other, that in itself will dispel the biggest barrier to U.S.-Japan communications—the idea of "Japan, Inc."

IS JAPAN A SNOB?

In late September of 1986, Prime Minister Nakasone made some comments in what he thought was a private session that traveled across the Pacific and irked the black and Hispanic population in the United States. Mr. Nakasone said that the Japanese were fortunate compared with Americans whose level of education is not the same due to racial minorities. His remark caused such negative reaction that the Prime Minister apologized immediately to the American people.

The Prime Minister may seem to have been careless, but in fact, it is very easy for Japan's leaders to say things that will not only get misinterpreted but anger foreigners. The problem is our language. We have imported many English words but not all of their meanings. *Smart* in Japanese does not mean having a good brain, but slender or chic. Likewise, a *mansion* is nothing more than a two-bedroom apartment house. By *intelli* we really don't mean smartness, but educational level. It has nothing to do with genes.

Nevertheless, the Prime Minister used a word that could be translated as the "intelligence" level of the Americans, hence it caused many Americans to think that he was comparing IQs and saying that blacks and Hispanics drag America's average down.

The news of reaction in the United States echoed back to Japan as a tidal wave. Most Japanese interpreted it as the whole of America rising up in anger. A Reuters wire read, "Nakasone quote irks blacks and Hispanics." It didn't say "Americans," but that is how we interpreted it. If we had a situation like this, it would certainly have been "Reagan quote irks the Japanese" and it would be accurate. We are simply not used to living in a multiracial and multireligious environment. We also do not have the same history as America where the pursuit of their rights by different groups has sensitized people to the importance of careful communication. Americans have learned to use or not use certain words and expressions regarding minorities and religions, for example. We have no such history, and this makes Japan's communications with the rest of the world and the globalization of Japanese corporations next to impossible. We don't even begin to understand the subtleties. So I don't think we should blame the Prime Minister alone as most Japanese journalists are doing. Any one of us could have caused the same problem.

The word *gaijin* itself means "outsider," an inappropriate word to use in today's global era. A derogatory word for gaijin is *keto* meaning Chinese hair. Even our Japanese-English dictionary translates it as a white man, a Westerner, for fear of a foreigner getting angry. But we all know it really means a hairy man, an expression taken from the Westerner's physical appearance compared with us, the nonhairy men. As a starter, I believe we should eliminate the use of "aliens" for non-Japanese, as is used at the Narita Airport. All non-Japanese citizens must carry an "Alien Registration Card" at all times while in Japan. This infuriates so many foreign residents, because it sounds as though we are really separating them from us.

We have many other expressions as a result of 2,000 years of isolation from the rest of the world. The world put up with our clumsy communication when we were insignificant. Now that we are on stage with America and Europe, we better act like and talk like world citizens.

This is more than a matter of cleaning up our "elevator language." We must watch ourselves carefully not to give an impression that we have a sense of racial superiority. There have already been comparisons in the United States between us and the Germans before World War II. We have tried to prove ourselves so hard that we tend to boast too much about our accomplishments in education and business. That is not only unnecessary today, but could be extremely harmful.

JAPAN, INC.—AN AMERICAN INVENTION

There was a time when Japanese-style management enjoyed a sort of boom in the United States. The Japanese were quick to rejoice, thinking that Americans had finally begun to understand Japan.

In reality, however, there was not that much to rejoice about. The praise was often double-edged. Americans tend to praise Japanese management in one of the following situations:

- When they want to get governmental protection and subsidies (against the Japanese).

- When they want to tell their unions why they have to fire employees and employ robotics and factory automation (like the Japanese).

- When they explain to the stockholders why their corporate profit is dwindling (because of those wonderful, patient Japanese).

In these same situations, American managers condemn the Japanese as unfair and cunning. The choice of arguments, that is, condemnation or praise, depends on the style of the person or company. So it is important to listen to Americans' praise with a grain of salt, caution, and suspicion. One thing for sure: Don't climb up to heaven when you hear Japanese praised from abroad.

Even when their praise was honest, what Americans and other non-Japanese actually thought was the truth about Japanese-style management was quite different from our insider's view. We know, for example, how little the Ministry of International Trade and Industry (MITI) influences the decisions of Japanese management.[1] But outside Japan MITI was portrayed as the mastermind behind Japan's economic miracle.

That kind of thinking, the product of U.S. scholarship, has laid the foundation for the proposition that Japan is a predatory economic animal whose calculating brain singles out particular elements of American industry for destruction. As this thinking goes, the U.S. sector is stalked and then set upon in a coordinated Japanese assault.

Even as venerable an historian as Theodore White has contributed to this stereotype. The article he published in *The New York Times Magazine*[2] recently (before he died in the summer of 1986) was an all-out attack on the Japan juggernaut. Recalling memories of World War II by beginning his story on the deck of the U.S.S. *Missouri*, he purports to show how the Japanese are now destroying American industry sector by sector. His metaphors are military. "Today, 40 years after the end of the War, the Japanese are on the move again in one of history's most brilliant commercial offensives." He quotes Secretary of Commerce Malcolm Baldrige: "Japanese export policy has as its objective not participation in, but dominance of world markets."

I saw evidence of this stereotyping most recently in a draft report for the government subcontracted by a prestigious university in New England. It argues that the Japanese government (read Japan, Inc./MITI) has identified machine tools as the next target in the United States to attack. Machine tools, it says, are too important to our economy to trust to foreign suppliers. We would be helpless if Japan sought to increase its bargaining power by stopping the supplies of machine tools to the United States after crushing the U.S. machine tool industry.

The report is full of misconceptions about where Japan gets its machine tools. Most are licensed from U.S. companies. What

---

[1]See my editorial in *The Wall Street Journal*, "Japan vs. Japan: Only the Strong Survive," January 26, 1981, p. 22.

[2]Theodore H. White, "The Danger from Japan," *The New York Times Magazine*, July 28, 1985, p. 19.

is more important about the report is its likely impact. It will be influential in circles outside the particular department in charge. Its publication could well lead to a new trade conflict that has been simmering until now.

The Japanese response to something like this is predictable. At first we will vacillate, due to complete ignorance of the origins of the complaint. Nobody will be able to understand why the Americans have suddenly lashed out at Japan with what will seem to be an ungrounded complaint. But since something will have to be done through diplomatic channels, a commission of Japanese experts who know something about macroeconomics (at best), but nothing about practical business, will be hastily appointed. These amateurs will meet and in due course prescribe remedies that don't get to the root of the problem.

In general, we will act as if we are dealing with fellow Japanese, mainly expressing regret that events took such a disagreeable turn (which in Japan in no way implies guilt). Not until it is too late will we try to find out why things flared up. We won't even ask a straight question: "Why the sudden outburst?" The main thing on our minds will be the need to smooth things over and move on to the next item of business. We won't learn that we should have talked things over at a much earlier stage of the conflict. As a result, we will run into more trouble of the same kind in the future.

This is why there has been no end to our conflicts. As soon as a textile agreement was reached, it was televisions; as soon as a television agreement was reached, it was steel; as soon as a steel agreement was reached, it was cars; as soon as a car agreement was reached, it was semiconductors. Now we are back to textiles. Truly preventive action is never taken.

The Japanese get especially angry that the textile issue, supposedly solved, is being brought up again, and ask why the United States is still complaining. But each episode in the conflict over textiles arises by a different mechanism. In nonhomogenous America, problems are raised by different groups, making it that much more difficult for the Japanese to respond.

Take the example of a complaint filed in September 1986 by the Rice Miller's Association (RMA) with the office of the U.S. Trade Representative (USTR). It claimed that Japanese unfair trade practices in rice have caused Americans to lose a $1.7 billion market entry opportunity. We have been growing rice for the past 20 centuries and have always been self-sufficient, which begs the question of why we should buy the American rice at all. If sheer competitiveness were the sole justification for market entry, then why shouldn't we sell more chips and autos?[3] That's what I mean about America being neither homogenous nor consistent. We feel that what Japan has said about steel and chips must be consistent with our position on autos. "America" doesn't worry whether the logic behind its push for baseball bats is consistent with its position on rice. So we have to deal with rice, and rice only.

That won't be easy. It will be difficult for the RMA to understand that rice is a religion for the Japanese. It would be even more difficult to explain that their pressure can deliver Japan to the Communist party here. Both USTR and RMA would certainly say that is a Japanese bluff. But it is true that Prime Minister Nakasone's Liberal Democratic Party (LDP) could lose if we opened up the rice market completely. The farmers still have some 25 percent of the voting weight despite their population weight of only 6 percent. Only the Japanese would put up with such nonsense as Tokyo residents having only one quarter of the voting rights of rural residents, typically rice growers. To explain why we cannot import rice, we must confess to the world that our democracy is a manipulated one, and that we really don't give one vote to one adult. That is such a disgrace that we prefer saying to Americans that we can't import rice. Most Japanese, particularly city residents, don't really care. But under the current political regime, if we alienated our mighty farmers, they might choose to vote for the Communist party, which clearly wants the rice issue to explode.

Most of us feel that it is bad manners for the United States not to remember tacit promises that it would never raise the rice issue between the two countries. Why pick on us? Why not ask the French to open their markets to California wines? Rice is not wine, say the Americans. It is merely a hydrocarbon, no different from wheat and corn. Remember, however, that it is not the Amer-

---

[3]As seems the case here, at least in the argument by Professor Charles Pearson of John Hopkins University, who was hired by the RMA to develop a somewhat simplistic elasticity model. The Economic Column, *Japan Economic Journal*, September 17, 1986.

icans who filed the complaint. It's an association called RMA. We tend to think that the U.S. government sent a secret signal to the RMA to go ahead with their complaint. But coordination between industry and government is not that good. There is no ESP between the two. Let's realize this, get organized, and explain to receptive constituencies in the United States why we can't start importing rice so quickly.

The American government itself consists of different departments—USTR Commerce, State, and so on—whose top officials each have separate jurisdictions. These officials aren't as determined or consistent as we sometimes assume. In Japan a ministerial official is expected to keep his position unconditionally once he has made a commitment. In the United States, if an official finds it uncomfortable in the Department of Commerce, it seems that he can find another job practically overnight in the private sector. (Recently, many are finding jobs as lobbyists for Japanese firms.) For an American, being a Commerce Department official may be just another job. Thus, the official's statements don't have the commitment we expect from the statements of Japanese bureaucrats.

In relations between Americans and Europeans, both sides make greater efforts to find out the other's background and hidden meanings. They understand each other and, even more important, they know they understand each other. When they find they cannot reach an agreement, they ask probing questions that reveal what really lies behind the other side's position. The result is an attempt to reach a mutual understanding even in the worst cases. They are playing the same game.

NO ONE WILL SPEAK FOR US

When a Japanese company begins to do business in the United States, does it encounter nontariff barriers? Of course. Countless obstacles lie in wait. In many cases U.S. regulations governing the sale of goods are extremely complex and totally unlike those of other countries. (America doesn't have all of its lawyers for nothing.)

For example, to sell piping in the United States each type of pipe must be certified in each water and irrigation district. In Japan, compliance with a single standard such as the Japan Industrial Standard authorizes the seller to operate nationwide. This difficulty, however, did not stop Japanese manufacturers from selling in the United States. We did not complain about nontariff trade barriers. We quietly overcame them.

American multinationals and other firms that have succeeded in Japan are also quiet. But those companies that fail to penetrate the Japanese market return home to complain to the U.S. Department of Commerce. The special trade representative then holds the kind of hearings where these firms publicly complain about their mistreatment in Japan (product inspection, non-tariff barriers, etc.). The testimony is published afterwards in the form of "fact books," and press conferences are held to lend greater weight to their tales of woe.

Naturally enough, companies that are successful in Japan are conspicuously absent at hearings. Texas Instruments did not condemn Japan on the semiconductor issue and neither did NCR and IBM on the high-tech trade issue. However, will they and other successful foreign companies in Japan do anything to clear up misunderstandings at the root of American criticisms? I don't think so. Because they have nothing to gain.

Their statements would draw attention to their success. The reputed difficulty of market access is, for them, a very convenient myth. It protects them. And they also don't want to advertise the fact that they took jobs away from American workers by coming to Japan. They might be criticized for exporting employment. Silence is thus the best policy for them, and we have to understand it.

Silence has been Japan's policy, too. But it is not the best policy. We must learn to speak out, or soon our trading partners will no longer be willing to listen.

Stating Our Case

The conflict over Japanese car exports to the United States is a good example of how Japan fails to explain and defend its position. Many Americans firmly believe that unemployment in Detroit is caused by the arrival in the United States of Japanese cars. It's not that simple.

In Japan, 670,000 workers, including employees of subcontractors and outside parts manufacturers, build 11 million cars a year. In Detroit, two million workers build 10 million cars. That's three times as many workers per car. Over the past 20 years, automakers in Japan have automated production because they found it difficult to get all the workers they needed. Detroit could have—and should have—done the same thing.

Japanese automakers do not owe their success to magic powers or any of the special advantages that Americans vaguely cite. It was not company songs, suggestion boxes, or other superficial aspects of the social customs of big Japanese corporations that did in American automakers. Nor was it lower labor costs, as Americans generally believe. By reducing the labor content itself, Japanese companies have made labor costs a small percentage of the total cost of their cars. Detroit's problem is one it created for itself: It has continued to build cars with under-disciplined people, not machines.

Detroit's difficulties began in 1974 when the first oil crisis caught it unprepared. But this warning was not enough to convince Detroit to modernize its production as well as its products.

If it had, the 1.3 million extra workers Detroit has with respect to Japan would not have been added in the first place. Over the last decade, the number of Japanese auto workers has not grown, while their output of autos has tripled. But for many years Detroit has hired (more) whenever demand grew and fired (less) when it shrank. The U.S. automakers now have the technologies to automate their factories. If they put them to use, there will be significant unemployment, regardless of the Japanese. But if the Japanese aren't careful, Americans will blame us for their unemployment. It is a lot easier to do so than to acknowledge past oversights.

In the last decade, practically every developed country has set up protectionist barriers to defend its automobile industry. For this reason, recent market shares of domestic makers have been extremely stable: 43 percent in Great Britain, 72 percent in the United States, 73 percent in West Germany, 67 percent in France, 63 percent in Italy, and 99 percent in Japan.

Each major industrial country has perfected its own system for protecting key industries. Outsiders trespassing in domestic preserves are warned off by alarms and find their advance blocked. The warnings explain why Japan's 1,000 cc and 2,000 cc passenger cars have not made much of a dent in the international market, despite their considerable cost competitiveness.

The largest lasting share that any of Japan's nine passenger car makers ever achieved in the Organization for Economic Co-Operation and Development (OECD) is Nissan's five percent share of the British market, although Toyota once briefly captured 6 percent of the American market. Even Honda, with its international prowess and 74 percent of its production exported, has not managed to top 4 percent of the American passenger car market, at least by 1985. By contrast, Chrysler had a 9 percent share the year it was about to go under. These facts speak volumes about how difficult it is to increase share in a foreign market.

Japanese automakers found their advance blocked in 1981, when their combined sales of the nine companies exceeded 20 percent of American market sales. They met fierce criticism at this point, and had to agree "voluntarily" to limit exports to the U.S. in 1982 and 1983 to 1.68 million cars, equivalent to 17 percent of the market and to 2.3 million cars since 1984.

Interestingly, however, the best-placed makers didn't have to cut exports. Each firm's ceiling was determined proportionally on the basis of its actual sales in 1981. Toyota, Nissan, and Honda, recipients of the biggest quotas because they had the biggest market shares, were able to do business in safety, certain of high prices with high profits during the duration of the voluntary quotas. Naturally they were willing to continue the quotas when the original agreement expired.

Today Detroit appears to be recovering, thanks to the protection afforded by import quotas. "Us against them" nationalistic sentiment is probably the reason why Americans for the most part accept the quotas on Japanese car imports as a justifiable step to protect their home industry in Detroit. Some even believe that the quotas are hurting Japan and benefiting the United States. But other Americans are beginning to realize that the reverse is true. Thanks to the import quotas, they are paying far more than they should for Japanese cars. A Toyota Tercel, for example costs about $2,100 in Japan but about three times as much in the United States. Japanese car manufacturers could sell their cars for far less in the United States, but they have no incentive. Lower prices should not increase sales because of "voluntary" import quotas. U.S. customers thus pay a high price for Detroit's protection. The import quota of 1.68 million cars imposed on the Japanese auto industry by the U.S. government necessitates a sacrifice—by the American people.

Judging from the height of anti-Japanese feeling caused by the car issue, it appears that Detroit has committed itself to a hostile relationship with Japan. But this is not the case at all. Convalescent Detroit has managed to improve the profit on its cars by buying parts at low cost from the supposed enemy—Japanese (and recently Korean) automakers and their vendors. Luckily for Detroit, there is no quota on parts.

American companies have also increased their ownership of Japanese automakers. American firms account for one fourth to one third of the stock of major Japanese automobile manufacturers and are usually top or nearly top on the list of stockholders: General Motors in Isuzu and Suzuki, Chrysler in Mitsubishi, and Ford in Mazda. Chrysler imports Mitsubishi cars and sells them as Plymouth Challengers. General Motors imports Isuzus. The top two auto giants in the world, GM and Toyota, now operate New United Motor Manufacturing, Inc. (NUMMI), a joint venture for passenger car production in California. Yet, the image persists of poor Detroit being unfairly attacked by Japan, Inc. American and Japanese automakers are clearly not implacable enemies.

Until recently the American press reported on the "battles" being waged in the auto industry without mentioning how Japan supplies Detroit with the ammunition.[1] Most Japanese are still not aware that any battles have begun. Statements by Japanese automobile makers are so bland they are barely printable. "We do hope we can reach an understanding . . .", and so on. It is time for them to learn the art of public relations rather than the just-in-time production method.

IACOCCA AND THE NEW YELLOW PERIL

Detroit has very skillfully manipulated American public opinion so that criticism that should have been focused on Detroit has been deflected onto Japan. It has succeeded in turning Japan into a scapegoat and avoided any blame for its own failures. Lee Iacocca, president of Chrysler Corporation, is very skillful at this game of mirrors. He has used the press to attack Japan many times. He gives virulently anti-Japanese lectures across the United States, beginning his talk by describing the serious state of the U.S. economy, then launching into a tirade against Japan.

His message: American efforts remain unrewarded because low Japanese labor costs rob Americans of jobs while the poker-faced Tokyo government maneuvers to keep out American products. Japan "doesn't play fair" and in fact commits trade "atrocities." He concludes that in order to preserve "the American way

---

[1]But the American press is catching on and beginning to puncture some of this PR. *Business Week* recently reported (October 27, 1986, p. 68), "For five years now, Chrysler Corporation has been promoting its American identity with such slogans as 'The Pride is Back' and 'America is not going to be pushed around anymore.' Yet among the Big Three U.S. auto makers, Chrysler is the top importer of foreign-made cars. It gets some 11.1 percent of its vehicles from overseas, compared with General Motors Corporation's 3.4 percent and Ford Motor Company's 0.7 percent. In addition, Chrysler's Dodge and Plymouth minivans, heavily advertised as examples of renewed U.S. competitiveness, are assembled in Canada."

of doing business," Japan must be told to desist or "we'll be forced to retaliate."[2]

Iacocca is famous as the man who put Chrysler back on its feet. Chrysler's recovery was instrumental in reviving the floundering American automobile industry. With his popularity enhanced by his best selling autobiography, some people now think he's the man to put all of America back on its feet. Groups are now calling for him to run for president of the United States.

This potential presidential candidate is, however, a man who would strengthen the Yellow Peril psychology that is growing in the United States today. At every chance, he attempts to whip up bad feeling by, for example, calling the United States a Japanese colony. "We ship them wheat, corn, soybeans, coal, and timber. And what do they ship us? Cars, trucks, motorcycles, oil well equipment, and electronics. Question: What do you call a country that exports raw materials and imports finished goods. Answer: A colony."[3] His words are chosen to provoke anger in American listeners, not mature reflection, self-criticism, or reasoning.

Japan remains defenseless against this deceptive and emotionally overcharged barrage. Not enough Japanese have sufficiently mastered the arts of communication to counter Iacocca's accusations. On the international stage, Japan is unarmed, unprepared—and mute. The only time we speak up is when our Prime Minister apologizes to the United States. If a potential presidential candidate is this outspoken and intends to downgrade the Japanese as a race, isn't it fair for us to say something about it? American niseis and sanseis are sensitive to such expressions as Japs and Nips and are careful to avoid these derogatory expressions, at least publicly. But they are willing to give a man like Iacocca a standing ovation when he labels the entire nation guilty of "atrocities." As a country and race called Japan and the Japanese, we do not react to remind America that we are also human beings and sensitive. Instead we dash to the

---

[2]Lee Iacocca (Speech to Commercial Club of Boston in December 1982). Adapted from "Revitalizing America: A Proposal," *Psychology Today,* February 1983, pp. 33–34.

[3]Lee Iacocca and William Novak, *Iacocca: An Autobiography* (New York: Bantam Books, 1984), p. 336.

lobbyists in Washington when there are some problems for us. We developed this habit about 10 years ago when, during the textile negotiation, we learned that American lobbyists are powerful, useful, and influential. Ever since we have become a one-track nation. In my opinion, the most effective and orthodox public relations is to communicate the facts and our true feelings directly to the American people, perhaps through high-quality journalists.

We need to make the facts known. But not by buying full-page advertisements in *The New York Times* or *The Wall Street Journal*. Such advertisements, whether they appeal to feelings or to rational thought, create the impression that the Japanese are trying to buy public opinion. People know that a full page in one of these newspapers costs a great deal of money and are suspicious of special interest groups who resort to such means of persuasion. The right way is to narrowcast to groups whose interests coincide with ours.

My McKinsey partner, Richard Foster, has written a book in America that describes how, when a major new technology invades an industry, the leaders of that industry lose their leadership and suffer greatly.[4] He describes how this has happened in industries as different as semiconductors, tire cords, and commodity chemicals. That is what has happened to the U.S. auto industry. Technology has invaded it, not Japan, and it has vanquished many jobs. Technology has been the cause of many trade disputes, not just the ones between America and Japan. A recent *Wall Street Journal* article on technology in the lumber business describes how it has exacerbated disputes between Canada and the United States. New high-tech mills have only 2 workers inside where there used to be 10. And one man with a machine can do what five men with chain saws used to do.

According to a study by the U.S. International Trade Commission, the United States produced about the same amount of softwood lumber in 1984 as in 1977, but the softwood sawmill work

---

[4]Richard Foster, *Innovation: The Attacker's Advantage* (New York: Summit Books, 1986). Fortunately, I don't see the kind of aversion to new technology among our Japanese companies that Foster finds in American companies. In fact, he points out how we have embraced new materials technology and biotechnology and how in some of our steel mills semiconductors research is going on.

force fell 25 percent to 89,133 from 119,553. The number of saw-mills fell 18 percent to 2,856 from 3,485 in the same period.

The loss of jobs and the closing of hundreds of sawmills have helped feed the U.S. forest industry's campaign for a stiff duty on Canadian lumber, even though Canadians also have lost jobs to technology. According to the ITC study, Canada's sawmill work force of 44,374 in 1984 was 11 percent smaller than in 1977, even though production soared by 20 percent.

Because of technology, some economists expect more layoffs and mill closings, even if a penalty is slapped on Canada imports.[5]

In September of 1986, the United States put a 15 percent tariff on Canadian lumber. One of its chief proponents was Bob Pack-wood, a senator from the state of Oregon, where unemployment among lumber workers has been high. The tariff may save a few jobs for a few years, but it will cost home buyers over $1,000 per home, according to the National Association of Home Builders.

Canada's trade minister told the House of Commons in Ot-tawa, "Today it's lumber—tomorrow it could be any number of issues. This is not the way to conduct business between the world's largest trading partners." The trade minister is right, but Canada will have to do what Japan must do—reach countervail-ing constituencies in the United States, not debate trade prin-ciples at diplomatic levels. It should start with the home builders.[6]

Technology will save industries and some jobs. That's more, much more, than protection will do. Nucor Steel in the United States is a good example. In the last 16 years, while all of the major steel makers in the United States were closing facilities, Nucor has built seven advanced minimills. It averages 981 tons per employee versus 347 for U.S. integrated producers. But Nucor is the exception. The history of American steel shows that when industries are protected, modernization slows or is nonexistent. Protecting jobs in steel has cost American taxpayers $80,000 per

<hr>

[5]Allan Bayless, "Technology Reshapes North America's Lumber Plants," *The Wall Street Journal*, October 16, 1986, p. 6.

[6]The United States's long-standing trade surplus with Canada has turned into a $24 billion deficit. You can bet that if this continues, protectionist pres-sures against Canada will continue unless Canada is much better at substantive and effective public relations than Japan is.

year per job. That's only the beginning, and Nucor's chairman, Kenneth Iverson, points out other costs.

But the delay in modernization and the cost to consumers are only two parts of the picture. The greatest hazard is the destruction protectionism causes to U.S. manufacturers for whom steel is a significant part of their costs. Because the American steel industry is sheltered, world prices on some steel items are $100 to $200 a ton lower than in the United States. This enables foreign manufacturers or American companies that move abroad to undersell domestic manufacturers. Automotive parts, oil rigs, farm implements, appliances, railroad parts, and numerous other products are examples of domestic products suffering under this handicap. In 1979 the imports of these downstream steel products were estimated at 5 million tons. In 1985 they reached an estimated 15 million tons.[7]

Just as in the auto industry, so in steel, the problem is not wage rates but productivity. If U.S. and Japanese wage rates were identical, the United States still couldn't compete. Technology has been the key difference. And more people like Iverson, as well as the downstream consumers hurt by protectionism, need to point this out, with our help.

Nobel prize winning economist James Buchanan is right—politicians are the "invisible feet" of an economy. They buy votes from special interest groups with "debt" they raise from other groups who will have to pay for the program on subsidy but who don't see this drain on their pocketbooks directly or immediately.

Despite there being so many fundamental questions about the U. S. economy, the Japanese government cannot score even one public-relations point. During 1985, for instance, the United States had trade deficits with virtually every major trading partner:

Country	U. S. Trade Deficit (Billions of Dollars)
Japan	49.7
EC	27.4
Canada	22.2
Taiwan	13.1

[7]Kenneth Iverson, "Protectionism Ensures Stagnation," *The Wall Street Journal*, August 21, 1986, p. 22. Semiconductors are the steel of the 1990s and users of semiconductor chips could be hurt as badly by the new commodity chip agreement between the United States and Japan as the heavy steel users were by the trigger price mechanism and other protectionist measures.

Country	U. S. Trade Deficit (Billions of Dollars)
Hong Kong	6.2
Mexico	5.8
Brazil	5.0
Korea	4.8

Even so, Japan remained the primary target of fault-finders. There must be something wrong with our government and/or ourselves.

THE MECHANISM OF MEDIA COVERAGE

Just as Americans need to know the facts about Japan, we need to know the facts about America. We don't. Too many Japanese correspondents in the United States have the instincts of travel agents, picking up bits and pieces of the kind of America that makes good posters and readable story titles: blonds in bikinis, street and subway violence, and wide open spaces, and, of course, politics. Instead of talking to Americans, they interview Japanese trading company staff on Reagan administration policies. Back home, their editors also know exactly what readers expect and select stories accordingly.

Similarly, too many American journalists in Japan tend to interview only those who can speak English. Currently, there are 12 reporters from major American newspapers permanently stationed in Japan, but only a few of them, to my knowledge, speak fluent Japanese, and even fewer can read and write the language beyond an elementary level. There are Japanese-speaking American reporters on the staffs of major American news magazines and wire services. Nonetheless, in many cases American journalists are simply not adequately equipped to conduct an interview about a complicated issue.

I've been told by some of them that editors back in the United States tend to distrust reporters who speak Japanese and know too much about the real Japan. They think that "old Japan hands" have "been in Japan too long."

My impression from frequent personal contact with many American and European reporters is that they sincerely want to write what they believe to be the truth. They are not inclined to support protectionism in either the United States, Europe, or

Japan and are always on the lookout for unfairness. They can be fair if they are informed. Therefore, although their fact-gathering methods are often less than ideal, the greater fault lies with the Japanese, who do not even attempt to provide them with accurate data and perspective.

If we made serious efforts to give American reporters the straight facts in an easily understandable form, they would not fail to perceive their importance and would make an effort to pass on the information to the American people. Put yourself in the reporter's position: Unless he or she is provided with readable information on a day-to-day basis, there is no reliable background data on which to base a story when the time comes to respond suddenly to a press release. The reporter consequently has to fall back on stereotypes about Japan.

For example, a foreign reporter is apt to see the Japanese rice problem in the following terms: Those responsible for the rice policy in Japan do everything in their power to keep the scandal under wraps. In the Ministry of Agriculture, Forestry, and Fisheries, the very mention of rice price supports is taboo. No amounts of prodding can lead them to talk about it in front of foreign reporters. PR people pretend to be out and everyone refuses to give interviews. They refuse even to allow their names to be cited. As a result, the story published in America boils down to a report that sources refuse to cooperate, and that no one shows any willingness to solve underlying problems.

The impression created by such reports is that coddled and unproductive Japanese farmers exert political pressure on the Japanese government to prevent the Japanese rice market from being opened to American competition. This only reinforces the myth of government–private sector collusion.

Japanese farmers do have a strong hold on our politicians, but at least we could try to explain the almost religious attitude the Japanese have toward rice. Or try to put the rice issue in context: For example, ask the Americans how they feel about importing wheat from Russia, or Argentina. Rice and inconsequential items like baseball bats make our markets look closed, despite all that we import from the United States, or despite all the success stories of American multinationals in Japan.

EVEN UNTRUTHS HAVE THE POWER TO PERSUADE

Henry Kissinger once said that public opinion has power, even when it's not true. In other words, public opinion does not always have to be accurate. Something can have public power even if it's a lie. Once it has power, it must be regarded as one of the realities of the situation and a factor in an extremely tricky mechanism. Given how many articulate people and weak companies are using Japan as a scapegoat, our present superficial responses will have almost no effect. Let's not respond in haste with apologies any more. Let's respond with honest, thoughtful arguments and facts.

HEADLINES THAT INVITE MISUNDERSTANDING

To maintain a profitable exchange of views between two countries is not easy, even when serious conscious efforts are made constantly. Sometimes, one side overreacts to unforeseeable events that go unnoticed by the other side.

Japan's weekly magazines are known for their flashy and exaggerated headlines, and are very likely, for example, to title a story on American trade policy "Reagan's Revenge on Japan!" or describe the arrival of Reagan aides as "Reagan's California Mafia Lands in Japan." Hyperbole is so much the weeklies' stock-in-trade that nobody even notices—in Japan.

There are, however, over 1,000 employees or contractees of the U.S. government in universities and embassies of the United States and Japan whose job it is to comb the Japanese press and channel information on coverage and tone to decision makers. Titles and many articles are translated almost literally. Imagine the impact of these titles on the people actually concerned, say, a member of the Reagan administration, characterized as the "California Mafia." How would the Japanese feel if the arrival of Nakasone's security staff in Washington were heralded as "Don Nakasone's Yakuza Meet the G-Men"? In just a week's journalistic production, there is enough material to fan bad feeling for 6 months, and the problem is not limited to the reaction of the United States. Chinese and Koreans are even more sensitive, and get the same treatment, or worse.

The tone of Japanese press articles on defense matters is extremely difficult to analyze and confusing for Americans who seek to pin down a Japanese approach to defense. The arrival of the U.S.S. Enterprise is greeted with noisy demonstrations and general hostility, and the editorials and columns of the press are constantly reminding the Japanese ("the world's only victims of atomic bombing") that atomic powered and armed ships find berths in Japanese ports. This does not imply, however, that the Japanese favor total disarmament. Many Japanese realize that our country uses American military strength to keep the Soviet Union at a respectful distance in a delicate balance of military power that includes very little Japanese participation, financial or otherwise. The Americans must have the impression from press reports that Japan is a very ungrateful recipient of aid.

In such delicate questions as defense there are areas, of course, where the feelings of the Japanese are difficult to put into words. But these are precisely the areas where we cannot expect people of other nations to understand our feelings. As is so often the case, Japanese self-centeredness raises a barrier to communications at the same time that it creates the need to communicate. Japan needs to communicate.

Japan is callously sowing the seeds of misunderstanding on the one hand, without being even slightly conscious of the fact. On the other, the Japanese are hypersensitive about inaccurate American press coverage of Japan. Not that any effort is made to remedy the misunderstanding at the root of these reports. To do so would require speed, timing, and organization beyond the capacity of individuals, and therefore, we reason, it ought to be taken up by some government agency. But that in itself may enhance the image of Japan, Inc., and in the end such orchestrated efforts may even have adverse effects. We must learn to respond as individuals. Then the medium will be our message: Japan is not an orchestrated economic machine. In our paternal society, it is usually the head of the house who speaks on behalf of everyone else. We unintentionally apply this to the country, and we believe that we have to have a single point of view when we speak up. That underlying psychology creates two problems: no response or delayed response, and the perception that we have only one point of view.

A YAKUZA SOCIETY

In fact, we often behave like Yakuza, or an underground organization. Some of us seem to assume that if a person is Japanese, he or she must think a certain way. For example, if one asks in Japan "Are you a Japanese?" it has come to mean "Come on, a Japanese shouldn't act or think like that!" In the United States, if one asks "Are you an American?" it is often simply a question about nationality; less and less so in Japan.

We have given the word *Japanese* an abstract, metaphysical meaning of rules and by-laws that govern the way we act and think. The myth of racial unity was fine when we were a small nation, trying to catch up with everyone else in the world. We needed it after the World War II when all we had was ashes and hungry people. The whole world would tolerate (or even sympathize with) a "family" getting organized to take care of itself.

Today, when we are the second largest economy in the free world, our kind of "mind our own business" and "we need your help but we can't afford to help you" attitudes infuriate people. It begins to smell, because we haven't fundamentally grown out of the old mold.

And while we may not intend to appear so, the world outside is beginning to perceive us as racially arrogant. Again, the problem is in part our language. In order to cheer ourselves over rough times, we developed many phrases and expressions that now cause problems.

- "We Japanese." There is nothing like "We Japanese" that could lead reasonable people into thinking we have totalitarian tendencies. It should be "I," or "We, a group of husbands in Japan." Despite our relative homogeneity, we are too diverse and too broad a country and people to be represented by "We."

- "Single race." We are offshoots of Manchurians and Koreans, and belong to the Mongolian family. We are the product of these bloods mixed with Polynesians and Ainus. We are no more pure than any of our neighboring nations. The idea of a "single race" was a convenient myth to cheer us up and to get the nation united in catching up with the West. It has no more meaning than the Americans calling their country "United" States.

- "Japanese brain." Out of curiosity and competitiveness we often want to measure IQs and other academic achievements against other nations. These racial Olympics used to give us hope. Some 20 years ago, a United Nations survey scored Japanese mathematics students tops among participating nations and we all cheered. But now we have gone too far. As James Fallows reports:

The Japanese public has a voracious appetite for Nihon-jinron—the study of traits that distinguish them from everyone else. Hundreds of works of self-examination are published each year. This discipline involves perfectly reasonable questions about what makes Japan unique as a social system, but it easily slips into inquiries about what makes the Japanese people special as a race. Perhaps the most lunatic work in this field is *The Japanese Brain*, by a Dr. Tadanobu Tsunoda, which was published to wide acclaim and vast sales in the late 1970s. The book contends that the Japanese have brains that are organized differently from those of the rest of humanity, their internal wiring optimized for the requirements of the Japanese language. (Tsunoda claims that all non-Japanese—including "Chinese, Koreans, and almost all Southeast Asian peoples"—hear vowels in the right hemispheres of their brains, while the Japanese hear them in the left. Since the Japanese also handle consonants in the left hemisphere, they are able to attain a higher unity and coherence than other races)

* * * * *

Tsunoda is still a prominent non-ridiculed figure in Japan. Whatever the Japanese may think of his unique-brain theory, large numbers of them seem comfortable with the belief that not just their language but also their thoughts and emotions are different from those of anyone else in the world.

The Japanese language is the main evidence for this claim. It is said to foster the understatement for which the Japanese are so famous, and to make them more carefully attuned to nuance, nature, unexpressed thoughts, and so forth, than other people could possibly be. Most of all, it is a convenient instrument of exclusion.[8]

---

[8]James Fallows, "The Japanese Are Different from You and Me," *The Atlantic*, September 1986, pp. 35–41.

While it is OK for us to be interested in how our language affects the division of labor between the left and right brain, it would make us look like arrogant fools to go any further. I know this is not the intention of Dr. Tsunoda, but we must realize that our kitchen conversation is overheard, nowadays, by many outsiders.

AN AGGRESSIVE VOICE FOR JAPAN

There are Americans who, though not "old Japan hands," are nevertheless relatively knowledgeable about Japan. When Japanese seek to inform Americans about Japan, however, they would do well *not* to aim their efforts at these people. The motivation to learn about Japan for most such Americans is self-interest. Through their Japan-area expertise, they can raise their standing in the United States. And of course, there is nothing wrong in this.

It is, however, completely unrealistic, even absurd, for the Japanese to count on these people to defend Japan's position in the United States. For one thing, even if they attempt to protect Japan's interests by exerting influence on the U.S. government, what they say might be inadvertently false or be couched in language that is detrimental to Japan in the long run. It is staggering to find how much Americans have learned about Japan from Americans such as Peter Drucker, Ezra Vogel, James Abbegglen, William Ouchi, and Richard Pascal, and how little from the Japanese themselves. I am not saying these scholars have misled the Americans. On the contrary. But this does not mean we can relax and not even try to tell our own stories to the Americans and our Asian neighbors.

The Japanese must rely on their own powers of persuasion and knowledge to make the real Japan known to the United States and the rest of the world. To fail to explain ourselves to Americans, our single most important ally, is to abandon any hope of really being understood. It is in our own self-interest.

The efforts the Japanese are now making are far from adequate. Articles in influential American newspapers and magazines, written in English by Japanese to clarify Japan's point of view, number only about 40 a year.

In the next year or two, Japan will at last become aware, and painfully so, of the inadequacy of its past efforts to communicate in an age of growing internationalization; that it is still unaware of elementary facts, is still unable to manage its own interests, and puts itself into high gear only when the mood in the U.S. Congress gets ugly. When the pressure eases, it puts its programs on the back burner, giving only lip service to the need for better communication and an organized information effort.

As things currently stand in Japan, who or what organization is capable of defending Japan? The Japanese External Trade Organization, JETRO, whose purpose is to promote trade, recently has been given the additional task of external relations. But this change amounts to a whitewash because it doesn't recast the structures that were designed to boost Japan's exports a few decades ago. JETRO doesn't have the capability needed to mount a full-scale publicity program on foreign territory.

The Overseas Department of the Federation of Economic Organizations (Keidanren), which acts as spokesperson for Japanese industry, is making attempts to speak out for Japan, but it cannot handle every issue, and tends to shy away from agricultural questions. For example, when Keidanren officers from the Daiei supermarket chain and from Ajinomoto, a company that is active in agroindustry, began to publicize their private opinions on farm problems, farmers retaliated by boycotting the products of both firms. Keidanren gave the mob these men's heads, rather than letting discredit fall upon both their companies and Keidanren.

Of all the possible candidates, the Prime Minister's office, with its ability to make decisions based on the general public interest, seems best equipped to be our spokesman. That does not mean, however, that simply creating a new section in the Prime Minister's office for overseas public relations will result instantly in a new "voice of Japan."

Instead, all of us have an obligation to forcefully counterattack organizations that have adopted positions and policies overtly antagonistic to Japan. We should do this openly, allowing the Japanese media to make an issue of it and amplify the public outcry. Just as Korea complained about passages in Japanese school textbooks that distorted its history, Japan should complain loudly and persistently when Japan receives unfair coverage abroad.

We can no longer beg others to make allowances for "special circumstances" prevailing in Japan. No more "Please understand, please understand." There is nothing to be begged for. Whenever special circumstances exist, they make our case that much stronger, provided we present the case logically—just as people in other countries expect.

We must become more conscious of the need to inform people of other nations of our positions and our diversity of opinions, and we must outgrow our repugnance for outspokenness. Until each of us learns this lesson, it will be impossible to entrust the job of communication to a specialized organization and Japan will remain a mute bystander to international events.

CORPORATE COMMUNICATIONS

Communicating one's position in a global economy will best follow from having *established* such an independent position. Japanese companies must become players on their own and not act as if their home country is a safe haven to which they can retreat for cover when times get tough. Likewise, the Japanese people must move away from attitudes of communal responsibility when it comes to our internationally active corporations. The commonality of interests and values, of joy and shame, that hold us together as a society must stop at the water's edge. As a people we may think of ourselves as descendants of the emperor, but out in the greater marketplace we are like everyone else, competing under the same rules.

When, for example, representatives of Hitachi and Mitsubishi were caught spying on IBM in 1982, the Japanese government refused to permit them to face trial in the United States. When the Hitachi story hit the newspapers, other Japanese firms refused to criticize Hitachi. Their guilty conscience, sympathetic unwillingness to add to Hitachi's misery, and fear that they later might find themselves in the same situation all kept them quiet.

They thought they could avoid blame in this way, but it didn't turn out that way. Japan appeared to be a wayward adolescent playing around in global commerce. Soon afterwards another Japanese firm was found to be responsible for similar serious breaches of corporate ethics, not to speak of violations of the law. By having tacitly covered for one, all ended up being branded, as if they had said, "Yes, we're just like Hitachi."

Japanese companies didn't anticipate when the incident erupted that by acting too neighborly to each other they would end up in the same boat—or cell. They weren't aware of the significance of their acts in the international context. Americans reacted to the incident as a hostile act. Japanese firms—all Japanese firms they suggested—had been using illegal means to obtain American technology in a way that would undermine American industry and aggravate U.S. unemployment. By being silent in the face of this suspicion, all Japanese appeared to sanction Hitachi's misdeeds.

We did not see this kind of team play and naiveté in the United States when the Union Carbide incident occurred in India. Nor would American companies have ducked an issue as important as industrial espionage.

What should the Japanese have done? If Japan were a nation with normal self-respect and regard for international opinion, the Japanese government and private sector would first have loudly condemned Hitachi's and Mitsubishi's theft of IBM proprietary information, if they were proven guilty. They would then have pointed out that Hitachi was, at bottom, a fine company with a tradition of public service and that the recent incident should be regarded as an isolated incident, and not be allowed to escalate into an anti-Japanese witch-hunt. If the same thing had happened to us, wouldn't we expect the offending foreign nation to do just this?

We made the same mistake in semiconductors. When Micron Technologies accused the Japanese semiconductor industry of dumping, the only evidence they had was, again, Hitachi. Apparently, Micron obtained an Hitachi internal document that suggested that dealers lower prices 10 percent when they encountered competitive bidding. To my knowledge, only one other company had a similar practice. So, when they were attacked, other Japanese companies should have said that they were not a part of the scheme. Instead, they got together to try to devise a response for the industry. Finally, MITI stepped in because the industry couldn't reach a consensus. This started a hair-pulling negotiation between MITI and USTR. Even though they know nothing about semiconductors, the two government agencies negotiated and decided what was good for the two nations. Most of the American computer industry opposed it and has said so publicly. Now, the European Community (EC) believes that the Japan-U.S. agreement is an international cartel and intends to break it. There is no end to it. We should let a corporation with bad trade practice be penalized. They will learn their lesson quickly. Let's not be "united" as an industry when we are suspected of espionage and/or dumping.

Collective behavior, when it comes to business, plays into the hands of the Iacoccas of the world who depict Japan in sinister, collusive terms. It also serves to validate the theories of the Peter Druckers and Ezra Vogels who have created Japan, Inc. and damn us with their praise for the supposed coordination between government and industry.

Let's speak out individually. In fact, the best of Japanese industry get out on their own to make their mark. Honda, Sony, YKK (the sliding-fastener or zipper maker), Canon, and Matsushita, among others, have developed concepts of their place in international society. They no longer fit into the common Japanese corporate pattern.

YKK virtually monopolizes the world zipper market, but its public image is extremely good. Its success is due to the wisdom of Tadao Yoshida, a man who had a philosophy of local production well before most of his competitors. Instead of exporting YKK's materials from Japan, Yoshida finds and processes all his raw materials wherever a plant is located around the world. He also believes in returning profits to employees and local communities. This is not a pious wish; he has made it a reality, and profitably.

People who are made aware of the YKK corporate philosophy through either its statements or its actions acquire a reassuring sense of familiarity with the YKK name on their zippers. Ignorance of Mr. Yoshida as a person would result in bad feelings toward its omnipresent products and Japanese goods in general. But only a few Japanese companies understand this, and are using intelligent, internationally minded public relations to create goodwill.

THINGS THAT CAN ONLY BE UNDERSTOOD THROUGH PEOPLE

Japan is still an unknown for the majority of the people of the world. Ignorant of Japan, its society, and the real aspirations of its people, the world might well conclude apprehensively from the global flood of Japanese goods that Japan is determined to dominate the world economically after failing to dominate it militarily in World War II. After all, how can people who know nothing about Japan be certain that Japan is not totalitarian? How can our country and its people be understood through anything other than our manufactured goods, since that is all they see? What other face could we show to the world?

To answer these questions, we need only reflect on what enables us as Japanese to understand the United States. Our clearest impression, set against an indistinct mass of facts and a vague image, stems from what we know of America's famous men and women.

We know America from stories about George Washington and a cherry tree (i.e., honesty), Thomas Edison and bamboo filament (i.e., creativity), and Abraham Lincoln and emancipation of the blacks (i.e., racial fairness). We know Americans, ranging from George Gershwin to Billy Joel, from Carnegie to Steve Jobs. We know about John D. Rockefeller and his oil empire, and of Alfred Sloan, the long-time leader of General Motors. We know about America's presidents, at least from Roosevelt to Reagan.

The fact is that its leaders are a way for a nation to communicate its identity. The existence of preeminent figures is essential to our knowledge of and attachment to other countries. Put another way, collective nouns and anonymity are not respected—only suspected.[9]

To a considerable extent, Japan remains an international unknown, a mystery for the rest of the world, because hardly a single Japanese is internationally well known. Faceless, souless Japan—that's the image negotiators believe and critics want to spread. It is not that we lack people of the requisite caliber. To cite the area with which I am most familiar, there are many industrialists whose stories are interesting and deserve to be told,

---

[9]This makes Nakasone's recent public stumble particularly costly. Even though awareness of him among American adults in the United States is about 10 percent (lower than that of Margaret Thatcher), he had begun to gain stature internationally and was perceived as an individual as well as a head of state. He appeared to be broader and more cosmopolitan than most Japanese leaders, and indeed no other Prime Minister has pushed us so hard to acquire an international perspective. None of his likely successors has or is likely to acquire this image because each of them is parochial and domestic in his views.

whose ideas, management principles, and personalities merit greater world public attention, and whose anecdotes would delight readers everywhere. In my opinion, the lives and success stories of Soichiro Honda (Honda), Kazuma Tateishi (Omron-Tateishi), Tadao Yoshida (YKK), and Genichi Kawakami (Yamaha) are just as vivid and entertaining as those of Henry Ford, Hewlett and Packard, and Steve Jobs.[10]

Their stories have not, however, crossed the waters that surround Japan. The world is full of Japanese televisions, radios, audio and video tape recorders, and cars—but few books on famous Japanese business leaders.

Matsushita Electric Corporation of America is a giant of American industry, with sales approaching $5 billion through such brands as Panasonic, Technics, Quasar, and National. Still, only a tiny minority of Americans know who Kohnosuke Matsushita is. The contrast with the number of Japanese who know about Lee Iacocca is striking. At the Harvard Business School I once asked students how many knew who Kohnosuke Matsushita is. Many of those who gave a hesitant yes to my question followed it with a question like, "Does he sell Sony stereos?"[11]

Soichiro Honda, once a competitor in motorcycle races and now in F-1 races, is the Thomas Edison of Japan. His engineering creativity and racing exploits would intrigue Americans. But Mr. Honda does not want to tell his stories. He believes that his products should speak for themselves. That in itself is a respectable story but in this day and age, that alone doesn't do the job.

Americans who use Casio calculators probably number in the millions, but few, if any, know the story of the four brothers who founded Casio together. They met every Thursday to talk over product development, and in a matter of years built their firm into a gigantic corporation known the world over. To American customers, Casio is still just a brand name, not a success story.

---

[10]As people who read the new book *Made in Japan* will find out. Akio Morita and Sony, *Made in Japan: Akio Morita and the Sony Corporation* (New York: Dutton, 1986).

[11]I told this story to Mr. Matsushita and persuaded him to do something about it. Subsequently, Harvard Business School has established a Kohnosuke Matsushita Chair. Professor Abraham Zaleznik, who is now teaching a course on corporate leadership, is the first to hold this chair.

Americans would be interested in many other anecdotes from Japanese industry, for example, the story of the Iue brothers and how they came to call their firm Sanyo ("Three Oceans"). (They thought that they had no chance to match Matsushita in Japan, but overseas, they intended to beat him at his own game. The name they chose signifies their determination to excel in overseas markets.)

Genichi Kawakami practices a truly unique form of management at Yamaha, whose products are developed in a competitive spirit of gamesmanship where one idea leads to another. First, Yamaha began to build furniture with the wood used to make pianos, then it developed electone organs, then FM sound generators, and finally synthesizers, amplifiers, and stereos. The pursuit of beautiful sounds led Yamaha into semiconductors. Its research has made significant advances in the areas of ASICS (application specific integrated circuits). Throughout, its goal was never immediate profits, but the maximization of music listening and playing pleasure. That's why they have thousands of Yamaha music schools to teach children how to play the keyboard instruments. A strategist might call this a "pull" strategy, but to Genichi Kawakami, it is an incarnation of his fundamental beliefs. In the course of pursuing this primary goal, Yamaha has become the world's largest maker of pianos and a major contender in the fields of electric organs and synthesizers as well.[12]

The whole history of Toyota, Japan's largest company, is the history of the Toyoda family. Sakichi Toyoda (1863–1930), the inventor of the autolooming machine, was succeeded by his son Kiichiro Toyoda (1894–1952), who started the family's automobile business. Today there are Eiji Toyoda, the current chairman, and Shorichito Toyoda, president and CEO. These men were aided by a handful of powerful entrepreneurs—Taizo Ishida, Soichi Saito, and Taiichi Ohno in production, Shotaro Kamiya and Seishi Kato in sales and marketing, and Masaya Hanai in finance. To be sure, Toyota is famed for the success of its suggestion box and quality circle activities. These, however, are not decision-making mechanisms but means of getting everyone involved in identifying improvement opportunities. Most of Toyota's major decisions have been made in a top-down fashion, or

---

[12]And sailboats, motorbikes, outboard engines, and snowmobiles.

at best by middle managers guided by strong directives from the top.

This is a story well worth telling, and one that certainly ought to inspire American youth, with their proven capacity to turn hobbies and other personal interests into the bases of new enterprises. Many other stories about Japan have universal interest and warmth. All that remains is to tell them, so that some of our most human and dynamic figures will be better known to the people of other countries.

Japan need not be bashful or overmodest; on the contrary, it needs better and more active public relations. But sadly, the Japanese lack even an accurate concept of public relations. An accurate grasp of our needs in this area is therefore one of the first steps toward increasing the world's understanding of what and who we are.

The Triad Worldview

Only 15 years ago Japan had extremely serious pollution problems. Policemen at the busiest intersections in Tokyo wore gauze masks to filter out airborne particles. But we didn't care about pollution as much as we cared about increasing industrial production. We turned our people into industrious swarms of busy worker bees whose average per capita income was equivalent to only about $3,000 in today's dollars.

Despite the oil crises, per capita GNP rose to $5,000 in 1974. Less than 10 years later, in 1982, it topped $10,000. The next year, it rose to $11,000 (Figure 5). Other countries with per capita GNPs above $10,000 include the United States, West Germany, France, Switzerland, and Sweden. England's per capita GNP is above $9,000 and Italy's above $6,000. Today, Japan's per capita GNP is $15,000, due primarily to the stronger yen.

In the process of this rapid growth, Japan rose from the ranks of the semideveloped nations, catching up and finally aligning itself with the advanced industrial nations, whose economic growth in the meantime was far slower. And Japan was the first non–Euro-American country to do so.

When a country's per capita GNP is $5,000 or less, Engel's coefficient (the percentage of income spent on food) exceeds 50 percent and very little disposable income remains. However, when per capita GNP rises to about $10,000, Engel's coefficient sinks to 20 or 30 percent and about 70 percent of income is disposable income. At this point, disposable income translates into considerable purchasing power.

FIGURE 5   Japan Entered into the $10,000 Club in the Late 70s

---

Japan's GNP/Capita Growth; 1945-1984

Real GNP/Capita; Current U.S.$

GNP/Capita (U.S.$)

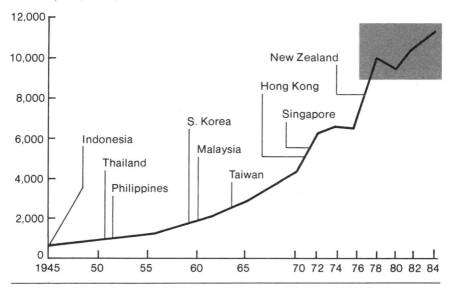

SOURCE: World Bank Atlas; Ministry of Health and Welfare; MOF; Bank of Japan (McKinsey estimates).

This is precisely what happened in the decade of 1972–1982; patterns of consumption and lifestyles were altered substantially. The first Japanese McDonald's was opened on the Ginza in 1971. At the time the idea of eating while walking was a disturbing innovation. Our mothers had always said, "Sit down and finish eating!" But in the 1970s, the Japanese began to see people walking down the street with food in their hands—and their mouths.

It was the first of a series of culture shocks, but this particular shock is over today. Young couples stroll down the street arm-in-arm eating ice cream and nobody notices. The generation that would still hesitate to do this is now a small minority.

Other things have changed. Ten years ago, sneakers were only worn during gym or recess at school. Adults wore leather shoes, and "exercise shoes," as they were then known, were not acceptable street wear. Today, people of every generation wear whatever shoes they prefer. The degree of tolerance of different expressions of individuality and of diverse styles has grown tremendously.

The simplest description of the 10-year trend in Japanese lifestyles is "westernization." Westernization has been in progress in Japan since the 1860s, but few decades have worked such deep and lasting changes in our daily lives as the 10 years before Japan's per capita GNP reached the $10,000 level.

Even toilet paper has changed. It was not so long ago that the Japanese used single sheets of crinkly rice paper taken from shallow box-shaped baskets hung in toilets. Before that, they used old newspapers cut into squares. Both have been replaced by soft toilet paper on rolls of exactly the same type used in the United States.

But toilet paper is just an example of how every facet of modern life, from clothing to food and housing, has undergone such radical change that the Japanese lifestyle is now fundamentally the same as in any other advanced industrial nation.

Rather than saying that Japan has gone overboard about Western ways, I prefer to believe that when income exceeds a certain level, lifestyles change in ways that were first experienced in the West. When people no longer have to work for sustenance and begin working to permit recreation, they spontaneously begin to choose similar and relaxed lifestyles. Japan is simply undergoing the same natural process that the West has experienced.

THERE ARE NO NATIONAL BORDERS BETWEEN LIFESTYLES

When we switch our focus from lifestyles to business in the $10,000 bracket countries, a single, incredibly vast market comprising surprisingly homogeneous needs looms suddenly into view. The wealthy industrialized nations of which Japan has recently become a member share, first of all, high disposable income levels. With disposable income having reached comparable levels, people's educational levels, academic and cultural backgrounds, lifestyles, and access to information in the urban centers begin to be the same. And as these cultural elements begin to resemble each other qualitatively, even such extremely subjective factors as demand for material possessions, ways of spending leisure time, and aspirations for the future become increasingly homogeneous.

Young Japanese in Tokyo's Harajuku, the mecca of the fashionable young set, wear styles and carry goods indistinguishable from those of California: Nike sneakers, L.L. Bean trousers, Fila T-shirts, Prince tennis rackets, and Lancel bags. The same fashions are found in New York City, Copenhagen, and Amsterdam. If roller skating becomes a fad in California, it soon spreads throughout the world.

These young people also share musical tastes. They listen to songs on the hit charts in Los Angeles. Japan's Yellow Magic Orchestra and other digital musicians have become popular around the globe.

Businessmen of the traditional stamp in Tokyo, New York, and Dusseldorf wear the same navy blue suits, Bally shoes, and Hermes neckties. The Mark Cross wallets in their pockets contain thin Casio calculators. They lunch together at sushi bars in business districts around the world. They choose between Technics or Kenwood stereo systems when they buy audio equipment.

In Japan, Mister Donut is not just a hangout for high school and college students; even families are regular customers, and workers from nearby construction sites come in for a coffee during their rest periods. In cities of modest size throughout Japan are signs for Kentucky Fried Chicken, Wimpy's, Baskin-Robbins, Shakey's Pizza, Denny's, and 7-Eleven. In Tokyo a tourist will also see stands selling David's and Mrs. Fields' cookies. Fast food has hit Japan with a vengeance.

In Japanese homes are bottles of Johnson's window cleaner, Pampers disposable diapers, Scottie and Kleenex tissues, Lux soap, Cheer detergent, and Johnson & Johnson BAND–AIDS.

Go to a supermarket in Japan and you will see Knorr, Campbell, and Maggi soups, V8 juices, Nestle coffee, Lipton tea, McCormick spices, Ritz crackers, Kellogg's cornflakes, Granola bars, Dannon yogurt, Borden's ice cream, Kodak film, and scores of familiar products from all over the world. Probably the biggest difference between American and Japanese supermarkets is the pickling paste and the dried fish in Japanese stores.

Japanese drugstores are also full of international brands: Wella shampoos, Nivea skin creams, Max Factor and Revlon cosmetics, Herb candies, Vick's cough drops, Contac cold capsules, Bayer aspirin, and many more. The brands that have managed to gain an especially good reputation for high quality in Japan include Cross, Parker, and Sheaffer pens, Louis Vuitton, Givenchy, and Nina Ricci handbags; Yves Saint-Laurent, Pierre Cardin, and Ungaro fashions; and Estee Lauder, Clinique, and Chanel perfumes.

Sporting goods stores are filled with racks of products by Adidas, Lacoste, Teng, Fila, Wilson, Prince, and Head. And over 50 percent of the skis used in Japan come from Europe. Their presence proves that non-Japanese product concepts are well received by Japanese consumers and have a lasting place in Japanese life.

Today, nationality is a nonfactor in daily consumption. National borders don't exist in the supermarket.

Added to these similarities is the quasiequality of road, telecommunication, power transmission, and sewerage networks, administrative systems, and other infrastructures. The telephone network is especially important, as it provides the basis for the development of high-tech industry. It greatly facilitates use of facsimile and teletext terminals and other digital and data processing equipment.

Roads are another important factor. When most roads are paved, a market is opened for such high-value-added products as radial tires and sports cars, which put real money into a manufacturer's coffers. They can't be designed or built without advanced technology.

As access to information becomes increasingly important to modern societies, it fragments markets into highly individualized segments at the same time that the overall needs of the world population become increasingly homogeneous. Ours is an age where *netsuke* and other items of Japanese cuisine or art barely known to the Japanese enjoy booms in New York City.

In advanced industrial countries, consumers' lives, lifestyles, and aspirations are becoming ever more alike as people the world over find the same things interesting or attractive and the same foods tasty. People live in similar residential neighborhoods, learn similar things at school, watch similar programs on television, and buy the same goods at the supermarket or department store.

THE TRIAD MARKET: 630 MILLION BUYERS WITH SIMILAR TASTES

This boils down to saying that 630 million people—the combined populations of Japan (120 million), the United States (250 million) and Western Europe (260 million) comprise a single market with common needs. I call this the Triad market. For the market researcher, their needs can be analyzed more effectively in terms of groups or clusters with similar habits and tastes than in terms of nationalities.

Consumer behavior today is more influenced by educational background and disposable income than by ethnic characteristics. Even religion becomes a declining "industry" in economies with over $5,000 per capita income. In the advanced industrial countries, the generation gap is greater than national or cultural disparities. People in their 20s are now interested in different things than people in their 30s, and each generation, including the increasingly powerful senior citizen bracket, has its own tastes that are the same throughout the Triad.

A worldview based on outmoded concepts of nationality and traditional antagonisms between nations and ethnic groups is not useful in today's trade. In fact, to dismiss it outright and treat the inhabitants of Japan, Europe, and the United States, or Triadians, as a single race of consumers with shared needs and aspirations is the first conceptual leap toward a pragmatic and productive businessperson's worldview. This is critical, because how can one be aware of new opportunities if one is unaware of new realities?

BUSINESS OPPORTUNITIES IN THE TRIAD MARKET

The first group of consumers to catch onto Sony Walkmans were the young people of California. Almost simultaneously, Walkmans become the rage in Japan and Europe. The fad spread like wildfire, as can happen with any attractive product in the Triad market.

The reason is that the market is homogeneous. As soon as the Walkman came on the market, consumers in the United States, Europe, and Japan simultaneously felt the need to listen to recorded music while strolling.

   Canon's AE-1 became instantly popular worldwide within 6 months of its launching. The Minolta 7000, an automatic focus single lens reflex camera, also won instant global popularity. People's needs, wherever they live in the industrialized world, are the same. When they take pictures, they want to take good ones, in sharp focus. It's not their goal to use a camera made in their own country.

   Five or six years ago, I used a calculator with a sound generator that permitted the user to play games when he or she wasn't calculating. I had picked up this item at an airport shop on my way to the United States and it aroused such interest that people asked me to get them one on my next trip. Recently, however, when I was showing off my very thin Casio calculator, which fits inside my visiting card case, a Dutchman smiled and pulled out his own, and pointed out that it was even thinner. The latest Casio had been launched simultaneously in all regions of the Triad, so that it reached certain parts of the Netherlands faster than a local shop in Japan.

   Today, new products circle the globe with the speed of a satellite. It no longer holds that innovations trickle down like a cascade or waterfall from the most to the least technologically advanced countries (Figure 6). This was true in the past; for example, it took decades for the custom of carpeting floors and watching television to reach Japan from the United States.

   For a manufacturer to assume that the need for its new product will spread slowly is equivalent to giving its competitors a head start on the global market. In the past, firms first attacked and conquered the domestic market before moving into overseas markets because they were certain that they could monopolize their proprietary technology and know-how for a considerable period. They also assumed that they could extend their networks through the world, provided that they spent the necessary time.

   Over the past few years, with the spread of technology, the increasing speed of its development, and the convergence of capabilities of high-tech firms, it has become impossible to be certain that one will have sole access to a new technology and know-how for more than a year. Moreover, the tremendous cost of research and development of high-tech products that appeal to consumers makes it impossible to recover the investment solely from sales in the domestic market.

FIGURE 6   MNC: Waterfall or Cascade Model

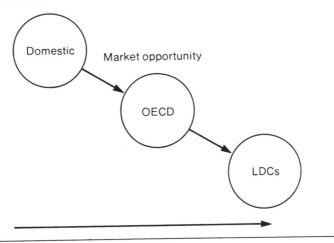

SOURCE: McKinsey & Company, Inc.

Firms simply must, from the very start, target the entire Triad market. They must launch products in all sales territories virtually simultaneously and have the capacity to promote sales on a global scale if they are to have any chance of success.

The British firm EMI developed the first computer tomographic (CT) scanner, a machine that made marvelous imaging applications possible to modern medicine. The Triad's medical electronics sales networks were controlled by Toshiba in Japan, General Electric in the United States, Siemens in Germany, and Philips elsewhere in the European Economic Community. Moving alone, first into the United States, EMI tried to establish its own networks, but failed. While EMI was building up its sales organization, Toshiba, General Electric, Siemens, and Philips were developing their own CT scanners. They soon pushed EMI out of the market. Market and sales force development takes longer than a decade. Even the most proprietary product will thus be outdated by the time a corporation can establish its global sales readiness.

The point, from the other side of the coin, is that product and service strategies targeted only for the domestic population are less and less likely to succeed. When planning takes the much larger Triad population into consideration, one's strategy holds together under a variety of circumstances. Universally applicable strategies and the resulting product and service concepts are more competitive and stand a much greater chance of success. This does not mean that companies don't have to tailor their overall strategies to local situations—that is what companies do anyway even in their home countries when they segment their markets. But now supranational segments exist in the Triad. And paying attention to commonalities across the national borders is often much more profitable than debating the differences of customers based on nationalities. Some Japanese youngsters can be "clustered" together with the Californians. That's the point I want to register.

CONSORTIA FOR SURVIVAL

For a firm with a good grasp of the shared needs of 630 million people and the courage to launch a product in the Triad market, it is essential to have networks that can deliver a newly developed product nearly simultaneously to scores of different points on the globe.

IBM and Nestle began to extend their networks, region by region, during an age when they had relatively little competition. Then the cascade model still worked. But ours is an age that no longer permits the leisure of waiting for a product to trickle down from the most to the least sophisticated consumers. The "sprinkler" model of product diffusion better meets the needs of today's markets. Manufactured goods must be deliverable at high speed from a central point as soon as the production "faucet" is turned on.[1]

To do this, companies have tried various methods of market penetration, including joint ventures, acquisitions, and mergers, but few of these attempts have succeeded. American or European joint ventures, acquisitions, or merged firms have often failed to penetrate the Japanese market, and the same applies to Japanese

---

[1] I explore the argument outlined here in greater detail in my book, *Triad Power: The Coming Shape of Global Competition* (New York: The Free Press, 1985) which was published in five languages (Chinese, English, French, German, and Japanese) simultaneously. I wanted to show firms to which I recommend a "simultaneous worldwide penetration" or sprinkler approach that it's possible in publishing to do what I preach in my consulting.

firms in American or European markets. The fusion of two corporate cultures is a difficult feat, and the contracts and other legal constraints binding joint ventures tend to hinder rather than boost their operations.

In an editorial for *The Wall Street Journal* a few years ago, I argued that "Joint ventures tend to get outmoded in today's increasingly volatile business environment since they are based on contracts that specify not only what companies can do but what they cannot. There is little room for initiative or for accommodating changes. As markets and competition shift, disputes over investment and resource allocation become frequent and frustrating . . . . If partners have to dash back to the original contracts rather than to a round-table discussion, you know they are in trouble."[2]

Presently the most pragmatic and productive method of expanding a product's market is the formation of a consortia alliance. Consortia usually involve the swapping of new products and models premised on the mutual inviolability of the partners' home markets. In this way, products resulting from expensive development programs can quickly be backed by strong sales capacity in the entire Triad market to ensure that investments are recouped.

When we look at the leading edge companies around the world, it is striking to notice how much fixed cost they have accumulated over the past 10 years (Figure 7). Increasingly expensive R&D cannot be variabilized, for example, through licenses, unless a company has its own strong products and also cross-licenses with others. The manufacturing process has also acquired many expensive robots and flexible manufacturing cells during this time. The sales force is a fixed cost a company has to keep regardless of how good a portfolio of products it has. In order to establish a brand recognition in the Triad that will actually affect customers, the minimum ante in consumer and office product areas is certainly $100 million. On top of all this, the information network of a company—its value-added network (VAN), local area network (LAN), and the like—are all fixed costs.

---

[2]Kenichi Ohmae, "Consortium May Loosen Up Stiff Joint Venture," *The Wall Street Journal*, March 11, 1985, p. 28.

FIGURE 7   "Fixed Cost Game" Requires a Corporation to Become "World Class" to Survive

---

FIVE "ANTES" OR FIXED COSTS

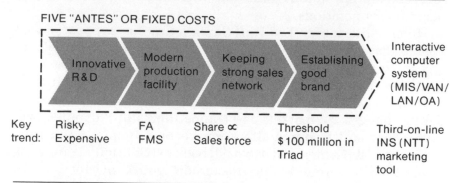

Key trend:	Risky Expensive	FA FMS	Share ∝ Sales force	Threshold $100 million in Triad	Third-on-line INS (NTT) marketing tool

---

Implications:
   Simultaneous, global penetration.
   Alliance to reduce risk/utilize fixed cost in place.
   SOURCE: McKinsey & Company, Inc.

There is no such thing as a half-baked computer. It either works or does not work.

All of these key elements of a company's business system have become fixed costs. They will add significantly to unit costs unless a company finds a way to amortize them with larger volume throughput. Even the Japanese market of 120 million people is too small if a competitor is a Triadian depreciating its fixed costs over 630 million people. If a company can afford to establish its own global network, that is certainly an option. IBM, Coca-Cola, and Nestle have all done so. But another option is to find partners who will help you to maximize the marginal contribution to your fixed cost. That is a basic principle in international corporate economics today. Triad consortia alliances that form global businesses are one result of its application. If a Japanese company has an unusually good product being developed in its laboratory, but not a strong network in Europe, it might want to find a strong partner in Europe. Hopefully, the partner will also have a good product, so that the Japanese partner can distribute it here. It has rarely made sense to distribute a strong product through a weak sales channel, but in today's global business it is close to economic suicide.

Similarly, if its production facility has extra capacity, a company might produce another company's product under its name, an arrangement known as OEM (original equipment manufacturing). If a sales force is capable of selling more than its product division can pump out, then a company might distribute its ally's products either under its own brand or the partner's.

The old Western model for international business was more or less imperial. A company invested in a joint venture and for a precisely projected return. For a number of reasons this model is not working well. Partners in a consortia alliance do not expect returns on investment (ROI), but they do expect returns on sales (ROS). What they are doing is maximizing contribution to their fixed costs, in effect getting more margins by tying up with allied companies that "replace" part of their business system. So long as the blood flows through the system, and they feel the warmth of their partners, the relationship will be fine. But it will have to be mutual. Instead of the old imperialistic model, which was aimed at conquest, we now see the Triad alliance model appearing, because it is much more pragmatic and it enhances global interdependence.

Today, trilateral consortia are being formed in nearly every area of leading edge industry including biotechnology, computers, robots, semiconductors, jet engines, nuclear power, carbon fibers, and other new materials. And we also see them developing in mature industries such as steel and chemicals.

Originally, few Japanese firms showed any interest in consortia. They tended to keep whatever relatively advanced in-house technology they had to themselves, trusting in their own capacity to expand their markets, even when they lacked adequate sales networks.

Ironically, some academics are now attacking alliances as another MITI-inspired plan to dominate the West. According to their argument Japanese firms use alliances to sap their partners strengths and then abandon them. American and European partners try to do the same thing, they say, but fail.

Part of this is just a new form of Japan bashing. Japan's JVC is criticized, for example, for innovating too fast for its partners Thorne-EMI and Thompson.

> JVC has constantly accelerated the pace of new product development, of improved product manufacturability, of transitions to new product generations (that is, to "slim line" VCRs), so its partners constantly have to catch up, retool, gear up for new types, reinvest in manufacturing, and—given the smaller volume they

make jointly for Europe, compared with JVC's own Far East production—incur permanently higher unit costs than JVC despite formidable efforts at cost reduction.[3]

All this has thwarted Thompson's plan to "learn from JVC's product engineering and manufacturing skills, in order then to reassert its independence."

Partnerships are what partners make of them. They provide contribution to fixed costs but they don't create fixed strengths. "Therein the patient must minister unto himself."

And partnerships don't necessarily last forever. They're somewhat like a marriage. In a world where currency fluctuations, technology, and partnering itself make strategies more slippery and uncertain than sustainable, partnerships—like competitive advantage—need to be reinvigorated often by *each* party or they will collapse, having made a brief but not enduring contribution to each partner's bottom line.

All this notwithstanding, companies are learning how to make partnership work both short and long term. Technology consortia recently formed to produce video tape, for example, have registered noticeable successes. Sony and the Matsushita group (Panasonic, Quasar, Japan Victor [JVC] and Technics) developed competitive products, the Beta and VHS formats, respectively. These were put simultaneously on the market in Japan, the United States, and Europe through both direct and joint sales channels. The Matsushita group gained a 15 percent share of the American market through its own sales channels. Then it conquered a further 45 percent share through OEM (original equipment manufacturer) agreements that allowed other companies to put their brand names on its products. In Europe, its partner Victor Company of Japan won a spectacular 77 percent share for VHS-format products.

In comparison to Matsushita's successes through the strategy of sales consortia, the Dutch Philips managed their video bid in their traditional fashion. Philips, confident in its own V2000-format video technology, planned first to develop the European market, to let American Philips conquer the U.S. market, and

---

[3]Christopher Lorenz, "How Can Japan Put a Spoke in the Wheels of the West?" *Financial Times*, October 17, 1986, p. 22.

then to move into Japan at a later stage. But while Philips was unhurriedly proceeding with its plan, the Beta and VHS camps formed consortia in the Triad almost simultaneously. Before Philips could react, shops around the world were unwilling to put V2000 products and their tapes on their shelves.

Many established European companies have misjudged the accelerating pace of technological diffusion. Philip's strategy would have worked very well back in the days of black and white television, or even in the beginning of the color television era. But today, companies have to be able simultaneously to meet the demands of the combined Triad population. The step-by-step approach no longer works. When incompatible products compete, as in the case of the VCR, it is particularly vital to arrive in advance of one's competitors. The speed with which a new product is delivered is a decisive factor for victory or defeat, and the pace of the race is still increasing day by day. Philips today has learned the lesson, and it took the lead in reaching an agreement on the compact disc player format as well as its video version called CDV.

Perhaps because we so frequently use the terms *international competition* and *trade war*, Japanese tend to overreact when foreign companies "threaten" to "invade" our markets. However, the real competitors, the ones that can pose a very serious challenge to the best firms in any country, are the second- and third-ranking firms of that same country. General Motors' biggest rival is Ford, not Japanese auto companies, and the same holds true in electronics and many other markets.

Early in the 1970s, Japanese color television sets were the most powerful contenders on the world television market because Japan's makers had made intensive efforts to upgrade production methods and counter the effects of the oil crises. They switched to integrated circuits, halved the number of parts, and automated assembly lines. The changes were very effective and enabled them to manufacture high-quality televisions at half their European and American competitors' prices.

Today, however, the industry is in the midst of a structural recession. Makers all over the world are finding it easy to make sets, but hard to make profits. Color televisions have become an engineered commodity. Both in technology as well as costs, there is not much difference between televisions of different makes because manufacturers all buy their key components and parts from the same global suppliers.

During the 1970s, Japan's color television makers were making profits and inroads into foreign markets. America and Europe consequently moved to protect domestic makers with import quotas and high tariff barriers. Japanese makers responded by increasing local production. Sony built plants in San Diego, Matsushita in Chicago, Sanyo in Arkansas, and Toshiba in Tennessee. But efforts to penetrate overseas markets did not allow Japan to capture the massive market shares that the United States and Europe feared they would lose. Sony has a 19 percent share in Japan, but only 8 percent of the American and 5 percent of the European Community market. Matsushita has an average 30 percent domestic share, but Panasonic and Quasar together account for less than 10 percent of the American and 5 percent of the European market.

Together, Japanese makers have a share amounting to 20 percent of both the American and European color television markets. In the United States, Zenith and RCA each have 20 percent shares, and no competitor has a larger slice of the pie.

In short, color televisions promised big profits in overseas markets a decade ago, but protectionism closed the doors to outsiders.

Now the tide of the times worldwide is again turning toward protectionism. When "invaders" from overseas gain a modest market share, protectionistic mechanisms go into action to impede further penetration, in effect slamming the door in the intruder's face. It will again be very difficult for companies to gain large shares offshore.

Many companies have been overly cautious about foreign competitors and not paid enough attention to *domestic* rivals who might be a bigger threat to market share. Ironically, one of the emerging strategies of international "competition" is teaming up with foreigners to meet a more dangerous domestic threat.

This has often been done in the United States General Electric tied up with Japanese and European firms in order to strengthen its position against Westinghouse. AT&T tied up with Olivetti and Philips in Europe and Toshiba in Japan. And despite the uproar over the "U.S.-Japan automobile war," it was General Motors that tied up with Toyota, Isuzu, and Suzuki, Ford that took over Mazda, and Chrysler that went to Mitsubishi Motors for a hedge against their American rivals.

HEADQUARTERS IN ANCHORAGE

To carry this idea one step further, in order for firms to gain in strength and grow with stability, they will be forced in the end to go global. Today and in the 21st century, management's ability to transform the organization and its people into a global company is a prerequisite for survival, because both its customers and competitors have become cosmopolitan.

Often this may mean establishing a presence and influence in the countries in which the company has major sales. Firms that are perceived as invaders fall prey to protectionism and import restrictions and find the doors to markets closed. But if a firm succeeds in becoming a true insider, markets will remain open to it, even when other firms nominally of the same nationality are excluded (Figure 8). This was the case with Sony, for example. When the outcry against Japanese televisions brought other makers to court to avoid the imposition of import quotas and levies, Sony was expressly exempted from these proceedings because it had a large assembly plant in San Diego. When a firm makes its products locally, providing jobs and paying local taxes on its profits, it can usually avoid being branded an outsider. YKK, mentioned earlier, is another good example of a company that has a philosophy and track record of becoming a true insider. Likewise, Nestle with a 70 percent share of the Japanese instant coffee market will be considered an honorary citizen, should something drastic happen to shut the foreign contenders out of the market. Both IBM and NCR are also good examples of insiders in the Japanese computer market.

Many economic experts are telling us to focus on our national markets. But a Japanese firm seeking world-scale status needs to do just the opposite—make itself independent of Japan. Heads of Japanese companies come to my office and say, "We're too dependent on exports. We want to establish a firmer base in Japan." When I inquire just how much of what they produce is exported, they reply, "Sixty or 70 percent." But assume that they are producing for the Triad market of 630 million consumers. Since Japan accounts for only 120 million, only about one fifth

FIGURE 8

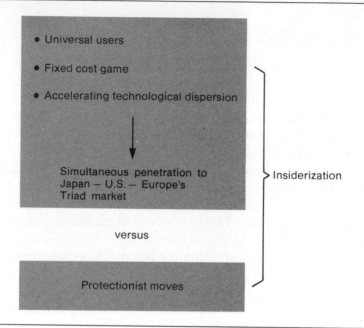

Note: JUE = Japan, the United States, and Europe.

Insiderization in each part of the Triad gives a company stability against discontinuous risks.

of their production should normally be consumed domestically. That leaves 80 percent for export. If a company feels insecure with a domestic base of only 20 percent, it's not independent enough to succeed in the world market. As in so many other areas we have looked at, the notion that ours is a special island apart from the rest of the world is one we have to discard.

Switzerland has a population of about six million—definitely a minuscule home market. Nevertheless, it is the home of some of the world's largest firms. Sulzer is an interesting example, because it is the largest builder of ship's engines, with a world market share of over 70 percent. But the only ship engines used domestically are on the tourist boats that ply Switzerland's lakes.

To be sure, some Japanese firms have been daring in seeking to excel in overseas markets. Sony was one, of course, but there are many lesser known examples. A small supermarket chain based in Shizuoka Prefecture, Yaohan, challenged the vastly greater Daiei and Ito-Yokado chains but failed in its attempt to establish a nationwide presence in Japan. In 1974, however, it opened its first overseas store in Singapore. Now it owns six large supermarkets there and is Singapore's largest food retailer. It's on its way to being a major factor in other ASEAN markets as well.

Fujitec, the elevator manufacturer, is smaller than any of its major competitors in Japan—Mitsubishi, Hitachi, Toshiba, and Toyo Otis. This has not prevented it from finding many customers in the United States and all over Asia. As a result, Fujitec moved its headquarters from Tokyo to New York in 1983.

There is no need for a company to keep its headquarters in Japan just because it began as a Japanese firm. In fact, I often say that the ideal place to locate a world-scale firm is Anchorage, Alaska, because it is equidistant from Japan, Europe, and the rest of the United States. Whether one actually moves to Anchorage or not, it is important at least to locate oneself mentally in a neutral position and not to overstress one's roots.

TRIADIC THINKING

The Triad is the advanced world. Eighty-five to 90 percent of all high-value-added, high-tech manufactured goods are produced and consumed in North America, Western Europe, and Japan. Of the roughly 10,000 patents registered in the world, 85 percent were filed in five countries—Japan, the United States, West Germany, France, and Great Britain.

What this means is that it is wrong to think of the world's countries as flat spots on a map; we must create a more three-dimensional view. Even today, the majority of multinational firms tend to take pride in the number of countries where they are present, but treat these countries as mere names, numbers, or red pins on a map. This "flat" approach will not guarantee survival in the face of tomorrow's global competition.

Ideally, a firm should be equidistant figuratively from the three strategic regions at the points of the Triad. When the firm stands above the map, so to speak, it forms a perfect tetrahedron or trigonal pyramid with itself at the apex. The third leg of course is the key developing countries, just south of its headquarters, or Asia in the case of Japan (Figure 9).

FIGURE 9   The JUE Tetrahedron

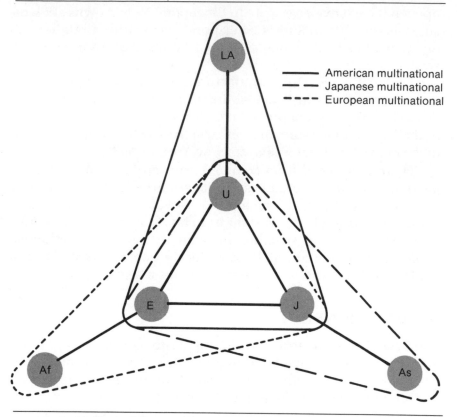

——— American multinational
– – – Japanese multinational
- - - - European multinational

SOURCE: McKinsey & Company, Inc.

A firm seeking to globalize should base its thinking on such
a tetrahedral worldview, not on a flat-map model, because it
illustrates how the three points of the base can be most efficiently
reached from the center (the firm). Seeking to globalize by expanding into countries of little or no strategic importance is simply unproductive dissipation of corporate energy. That means
that companies should be far more selective with their investments in developing countries. In order to hedge against exchange rate uncertainties, a Japanese corporation might choose
to have three locations for production in the Triad—Japan, EC/
USA, and Asian NICs. This is a rather new but important phenomenon. As a consequence of the extreme volatility in the ex-

change rate between the U.S. dollar and the Japanese yen (and other major European currencies), global competitors are now finding NICs as their preferred production sites. For all practical purposes, one can treat the NICs as America's home market since their currencies are normally pegged against the dollar.[4]

This notwithstanding, however, it is vital for a firm to become an insider in each of the Triad regions. Failure in any one would be like losing one leg of a tripod, with a consequent loss of stability.

Transforming branches of the enterprise into insiders at overseas locations through one's own effort, or indirectly through effective tie-ups with local firms, is now a matter of corporate life or death. Today's Triad market simply has no place for intruders.

FINE–TUNING PRODUCT CONCEPTS

The reality of shared tastes does not mean that a product will necessarily succeed worldwide without adjustments for different countries. Furthermore, the degree of adjustment necessary will vary greatly depending on the type of product.[5]

The same product concept without any variation will serve very well, the world over, in the case of cameras, watches, radio-cassette tape recorders, Walkmans, and so on, but it is always necessary to adjust concepts applied to stereo systems and televisions.

Japanese and European audiophiles generally prefer compact component stereos, which do not sell well in the United States. Americans like big, solid speakers and amplifiers, which, to them, continue to be the mark of high quality. Germans like the color orange and also like to see functional symbols on their equipment, such as double arrows to indicate fast rewind.

In televisions, also, Americans prefer big screens in big cabinets that sit directly on the floor. But Japanese houses are generally small, and the Japanese view their sets from an average distance of less than six feet. Big screens look fuzzy from up

---

[4]See my editorial, "Rethinking Global Corporate Strategy," *The Wall Street Journal*, April 29, 1985, p. 22.

[5]Ohmae, *Triad Power*, pp. 118–93. Degree of Localization.

close (although the coming of high-definition televisions may change the "picture").

Rice cookers are subject to very strong regional preferences. Most are sold in Japan, China, and Taiwan. But in these countries, they are expected to cook rice in different ways. The Japanese like a moist, sticky rice, the Chinese an almost dry rice, and Arabs demand that their rice have a scorched crust.

How well a company can respond to these variations is an extremely important factor for ensuring the product's success. Most companies, however, find it difficult to balance between localization and globalization needs, and they tend to think on either extreme of the scale. The reality is neither, and companies have to develop a feel for the optimum balance point by moving their people around as well as by using sound analyses.

PLAYING CHINESE TELEPHONE WON'T WORK IN PRODUCT DESIGN

This ability to fine-tune products is dependent, of course, on accurate knowledge of lifestyles and tastes in different regions. Such knowledge cannot be obtained from market research data alone. Designers must pack their bags and go to the target area for hands-on experience of other cultures.

In Japan, it's hard to find a piano that's not black. Pianos were used in Japanese schools long before they became common in homes, and this firmly established the image of the black piano. But in other countries, not everybody likes a black piano. Americans and Europeans think of a piano as a piece of furniture and order ones that are mahogany, rose, and so on, to match interiors of their homes. Furthermore, they expect the wood to be well finished. Japanese piano makers would not have succeeded in exporting to the rest of the world if they had stuck to a local product concept. They realized this after they sent people abroad to find from first-hand experience what people expected.

You can't design for an American living room if you have never been in one. What applies to pianos also applies to stereo equipment. A Japanese audio designer can have no idea of the space that his machine will occupy and how it will be used unless he visits other countries. Speakers will look like dwarfs placed beside the kind of big cabinets that Americans like. Globally conceived products must take these factors into account.

Nor can you design for young people without spending a lot of time in California. Many Japanese manufacturers, however, are still unaware that they must send their designers abroad if they want universally applicable designs. I once heard of an audio maker where the product planning process was reminiscent of "Chinese telephone," the game where children get in a circle of 10 to 20 and whisper a message to the person next to them, saying, "Pass it on." Local dealers compiled lists of desiderata, foreign offices collected these lists and sent them to people in the manufacturing division at international headquarters, who passed the information on to the planning section in the sales division. The planning section drafted a plan based on this information and sent it to the chief designer at the tail of the chain.

Each person in the chain summarized the information in his own fashion, and the message that eventually reached designers was often incomprehensible. It would have been a miracle if by this process designers created anything that managed to satisfy local consumers.

It's logical to seek global concepts and products from globe-trotters. Designers must be sent out to see the world with their own eyes. Regardless of criticism from their fellows that they spend half the year on vacation, they must have hands-on experience if they are to adapt products to real needs. The cost of this is a negligible fraction of what is spent on advertising and other steps in product development. My ex-McKinsey colleagues, Tom Peters and Bob Waterman, wrote that one of the keys to becoming an excellent company is managing by walking around (MBWA).[6] I might add that the key to becoming a Triad power is to MBWA around the world (Figure 10).

TRIAD CITIZENS

My message is simple: We have a lot to learn about doing business in the world. When the Daiichi-Kangyo Bank became the largest in the world, we all cheered. It was typical of our parochialism. We still behave sometimes like foreigners trying to conquer other companies and country markets. We give ammunition to the Malcolm Baldriges of the United States when we do so. We are not

---

[6]Thomas Peters and Robert Waterman, *In Search of Excellence: Lessons from America's Best-Run Companies* (New York: Harper & Row, 1982).

FIGURE 10 World into Triad Power, through "Anchorage"
Perspective!

Role of Headquarters

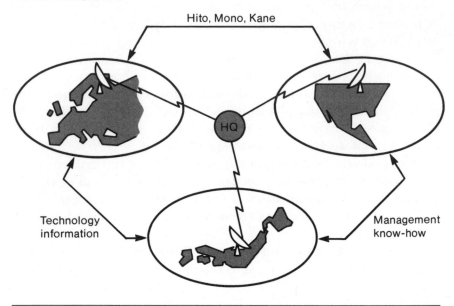

Note: Management by Walking Around the World (MBWAW) has become the key
to success!

SOURCE: McKinsey & Company, Inc.

in some Olympic business games. There are no medals to bring
home, no gold to horde.

We need to respect the necessity to put down the corporate,
not country, flag in the lands in which we operate, and be responsible to all customers—not just customers at "home." For
the true multinational, home is Alaska. And we have examples
of this—many Swiss corporations, Coca-Cola, IBM, Xerox, Citi-
corp, and certainly Honda, Matsushita, Yamaha, and YKK. They
all operate as good corporate citizens in the lands in which they
operate. In some cases they dominate the market, but there is no
outcry. They are well regarded, even special. In Singapore, where
job-hopping is normal, Matsushita has high levels of loyalty.
They all realize there is no room for parochialism in international
business. And it is clear from them that we don't need to lose
our identity to operate as world-class citizens.

CHAPTER SIX

Communications between Companies

If access to networks that reach every point in the Triad is a necessity for corporate survival, then firms will have to acquire new means of communication in order to make allies of foreign companies and become truly global enterprises themselves. Whether they form consortia or joint ventures or stretch themselves across the Triad, a prerequisite for an international firm will be the ability to speak a common language within itself and with its partners.

Corporate cultures are usually more individualistic than is generally believed. And when two conflicting corporate cultures come into contact, it can be extraordinarily difficult to establish communication between them.

It is, of course, partly a question of language. Firms, even in the same industry and in the same country, frequently assign different meanings to many basic words. For example, one company may use the word *budget* in the literal sense, to mean a framework for expenditures, whereas another company may use it to mean a type of planning. In some companies, talk of "mid-term planning" may refer to programs commencing tomorrow, whereas in others it may refer to plans at the stage of rough drafts of vague ideas.

Imagine, for example, that someone closes a meeting between two firms with the words, "OK, we'll do it next year. I'll make sure it gets in the budget." Depending on the listener's use of the word *budget*, this statement will be interpreted either as "Beyond any reasonable doubt, they'll go ahead with the plan." Or, just the opposite: "Whether they'll go along with us is iffy. Their putting it in the budget is no guarantee of anything." What was intended to dispel any doubt can have the opposite effect of creating uncertainty.

In-house word usage is often based on no common criteria, and no dictionaries are available for reference when you are in doubt about exact meanings. The language of corporate cultures can thus be a major stumbling block, hopelessly bogging down for example, negotiations between firms, even Japanese firms that to all appearances "speak the same language." The problem is aggravated, of course, at the international level.

Accounting procedures also vary markedly from one firm to the next. In some companies, divisions that lose money one year must make up the deficit the next. In fact, most divisions of blue-chip companies operate as independent profit centers. But others start with a clean slate at the beginning of every accounting period.

If two companies with different accounting systems begin to work together, the situation can become complicated. One side will be faced with tough decisions about whether to run a temporary deficit or to unload inventories to carry business over into the next term, while the other will be relatively unconcerned about year-end results.

Until the need for intercorporate communication and coordination arises, no attention is paid to these differences. Then, when trouble arises, often from the most unexpected quarters, it is not easy to fix.

Two Japanese banks operating in similar fields, the Daiichi Bank and the Kangyo Bank, merged more than a decade ago. To this day, however, all posts in the Daiichi-Kangyo Bank including the presidency are assigned alternatively, first to people originally from one bank, then to people originally from the other. In the case of Nippon Steel Corporation and Mitsubishi Heavy Industries, which were also formed by mergers, the firms that merged to create them had been a single firm before the war and were broken up by the Allied Occupation authorities after the war as part of their policy of dismantling *zaibatsu*. Their mergers thus amounted to reunifications following only 20 years of separation. But two decades were enough to allow separate corporate cultures to form. Notwithstanding the relative success with which these two companies remerged, the number of people from each of the respective premerger firms who reach top executive positions each year remains a matter of in-house concern, even today. There is still intercultural competition.

These communications problems are modest, however, compared to the problems the Japanese have encountered overseas. We have become expert at exporting domestically produced manufactured goods to the world market, but the times no longer allow makers to put products on world markets without globalizing their concepts and strategies. This means transferal overseas of capable people as well as manufacturing, marketing, and servicing products. Unfortunately, the increase in the number of companies that take internationalization seriously has been accompanied by an increase in the number of foreign failures or near-failures. Typically, Japanese firms are unable to take decisive action through their joint ventures with American and European firms. Clumsy relations with local production staff and inadequate knowledge of local government systems and social customs lead to conflicts with partners. This friction is avoidable and could be eliminated by better communications and interpersonal skills.

The need to globalize encompasses afterwork attitudes as well as products. Firms will not be able to succeed in international markets if their employees regard an evening of noisy drinking and singing in a Ginza-like bar as the high point of their cultural life. We don't know how to behave in international circles. We make "ugly Americans" in Europe look polished. Half the time we don't even know we look foolish. Two thousand years of isolation have made us schizophrenic. We devour Big Macs and wear expensive suits, but Yoko Ono embarrasses us.

People who have been brought up in the hermetically sealed cultural environment of Japan must make a strong conscious effort to become more international. Too often Japanese companies emphasize the easy part of local production—finance, products, and other hardware—and delay the crucial task of finding good people with the necessary qualifications. In fact, this may be the greatest weakness of Japanese firms today—their inability to find and retain good people for overseas assignments.

DIFFERENCES IN STYLE

American-Japanese consortia will not work if we don't realize that Japanese and Americans assert themselves in different ways. Most Japanese are unaware of this and, for that matter, so are Americans.

My impression of the United States is of a composite society, a mixture of ethnic groups, among which understanding is impossible unless people assert themselves. And self-assertion is dependent on self-expression. In the United States, public speaking is often part of the high school curriculum. Students take courses to learn how to express their point of view to other people.

But in Japan, to say, "ano hito wa, mono wo hakkiri yu ne!" (literally: "that person says things clearly") is a disparagement, equivalent to saying that he or she goes too far and is difficult to deal with.

In Japan, we don't teach children how to present their point of view. This is characteristic of our homogenous society, where people feel they understand each other without having to be assertive.

Interestingly, in America's upper class, for example, among the executives of big corporations, communication patterns are different. A sense of nonverbal communication plays an important role. Even in America, in tightly knit groups and among people of the same educational level with the same thought patterns, people understand each other without recourse to memos or long discussions, and this ability is regarded as an important asset.

Is it possible for Japanese to communicate exactly what they are thinking, with the same shades of meaning, to Americans? I think it is, but certainly with great difficulty.

BICULTURAL CONSIGLIERE

Japanese businessmen sometimes use English in their business dealings, but their command of English is tenuous. There are few Japanese speakers of English who are able to distinguish the subtle implications of different phrasings and use them appropriately. Japanese-American relations are going to create an increasing number of situations where verbal delicacy is called for. The problem is even more acute because the only Japanese likely to understand these shades of meaning and polite phrases are those who have learned them through painful trial and error, working for a big American or British company. Unfortunately, these Japanese are unlikely to gain enough respect in Japanese society to be allowed to fill an important role as bicultural communicators.

Successful international firms operating in both America and Japan always seem to have one or two people in key positions who work to facilitate communications between the two countries. At Sony and Matsushita in the United States, and at IBM and Fuji-Xerox in Japan, for example, certain individuals serve as mediators or in-depth interpreters.

Japanese firms that try to penetrate the American market without anyone to play this role of bicultural bridge have no choice but to take every step on the basis of a written contract. The result is almost certain to be frustration and failure of the overseas venture.

Successful firms always find a mediator in their organizations before they begin trying to establish operations or find a partner. This person is able to give Americans the straight answers and clear explanations they demand, and to provide Japanese with information and suggestions in acceptable form. Reconciling the needs of the two parties is not an easy task. The mediator must know what underlies the mental processes and group behavior of each side, how reactions to certain situations are likely to be expressed, and what the closest verbal or gestural equivalent is in the other language.

Under most circumstances, a word-for-word translation into English from Japanese is inadequate. Direct translation ignores differences in the mental processes and psychologies that are at the basis of language. What you end up saying with this approach is generally not what you mean. Many of the delicate but crucial parts of your message are likely to be misunderstood. The important thing is to go beyond a mechanical verbal message and focus what you say on the psychology of the other party.

Translation assumes the existence of equivalent terms in the other language used in equivalent situations in the culture. In most European languages, for example, the meaning of "I love you" does not change much in translation, because the context in which this phrase is used does not vary much among the countries of Europe. But in Japan, few would use the word-for-word equivalent of "I love you," although it is linguistically possible. Instead, a man would be likely to say, "Let's live together," or might even take understatement to a further extreme: "You know, I don't dislike you . . . ," or "Could you scratch my back?" At a recent press conference of a famous movie star getting married, the bride-to-be said she decided to marry him when he asked her, "Would you wash my briefs?" Now if you said that in any other country, you'd have a big slap in your face!

In general, negotiations in America begin with a period of what might be described as preliminary ice melting and skirmishing, although this depends on the situation and the people involved. The purpose of these preliminaries is to determine what sort of language the other side is receptive or sensitive to.

Some Japanese, for example, intensely dislike the term *strategy*. They think the word has connotations of trickery and foul play, and in their presence it is best to speak instead of plans, projects, and programs. The preliminary skirmish provides a chance to talk about things outside of the scope of negotiation to judge the character, mind-set, and basic values of one's counterparts.

The Japanese generally are suspicious of language and are immediately on their guard when someone says, "for example," "in which case . . . ," and "in the unlikely event that. . . ." They feel that to mention something unpleasant is to invite it to happen. They are afraid that if they suggest something that they don't want to happen, the other side will follow up on it.

But people brought up using English use the expression "what if" very freely. They are much more comfortable with dialectical reasoning. Japanese should make a conscious effort during negotiations to use similar expressions. "For example," "in which case . . . ," "let us just assume for a moment that . . . ," and "we hope it won't happen, but what if. . . ." These expressions enable one to judge the receptiveness of the other party.

The best mediators are Japanese who have lived in the United States or another English-speaking country long enough to learn from personal experience how non-Japanese think, but not so long as to lose their identity as Japanese. When they return to

Japan, they find themselves at odds with the attitudes of other Japanese towards non-Japanese, but realize that they, too, used to feel the same way. Their experience has given them added insights.

Bicultural experience is necessary, but by itself is insufficient. Some Japanese with foreign experience end up becoming more western than a Westerner, and are unable to readjust to Japanese ways. These people are shunned by the Japanese as *de facto* foreigners or classified as "smell of butter" instead of "soy sauce" and "miso soup." On the other hand, other Japanese live overseas for 10 or 20 years without ever adjusting to their adopted home, and continue to see things through Japanese eyes. Neither is good as a mediator.

Only Japanese with enough flexibility to adapt to other ways but a sufficiently strong identity to remain Japanese at heart are able to be mediators between Japan and the rest of the world. Neither their birth nor their overseas experience are so binding that they cannot escape their influence. Their strength lies in being able to draw from both experiences. The result is an entirely new species, a type of mutant with hybrid vigor. Unfortunately, we have only a half dozen of these today, far too few to bridge the many economic, political, and cultural gaps between Japan and the United States, let alone between Japan and Asia, and between Japan and Europe.

COMMON GROUND AND HONESTY

Business talks usually go very well between a firm in one country selling a product with a solid market share and a firm in another country that can't hide its impatience to have the other firm's product. In areas such as aviation and space industries, for example, where the United States is far ahead of the competition, relations between American and Japanese partners are remarkably unstrained.

Recently, however, there are more cases where Japanese and American firms are almost neck and neck. Now it is much less unusual for the rising standing of a Japanese firm to rival that of its American competitor or potential partner. The Japanese firm must consequently play more often the role of the strong party in negotiations, but it is not very good at doing this. Both sides struggle in this case to find expressions to accommodate, in bi-lateral negotiations and other communications, the delicate changes that have taken place in the balance of power.

Similar problems have arisen between American and Euro-pean firms, but they at least share Western culture and have similar ways to express shades of meaning, persuade opponents, and lay the basis for an agreement. Discussions tend to be carried out on roughly the same terms.

In Japanese-U.S. or Japanese-European relations, however, the thought patterns, the art of persuasion, and the mechanisms of consensus formation all differ so radically that talks frequently lead only to misunderstandings, frustration, and ill-feeling. Both sides soon abandon any attempt to treat the other party with any delicacy and attribute the failure to racial differences or pre-meditated evasion. We know that a smile on a Japanese negotiator is probably an expression of goodwill and/or an attempt to hide embarrassment, but Westerners often interpret it as a sign of something hidden or sneaky.

At the next stage of discussion, the gap widens and talks begin to be held on the premise that an understanding will not and cannot be reached. With both sides going to the bargaining table in this frame of mind, negotiation is certain to be sterile.

The Japanese believe that all Americans are as tough as Robert Strauss in negotiations. American negotiators arrive with full powers and want to get everything settled in short order. Their methods remind Japanese of the trade treaties with America that the Japanese were forced to sign by Commodore Perry immedi-ately after Japan (unwillingly) opened its ports to the rest of the world in the 1860s. Many Japanese feel that every treaty or con-tract signed since then has foisted disadvantageous conditions on them.

The Americans have the opposite impression, of course. They think that the Japanese are master negotiators and manage always to get their way. As Americans see it, the Japanese arrive in a group and interrupt proceedings upon the slightest pretext for consultations, from which they always return with hard-line pro-posals. Americans genuinely dislike this style of business talks.

On the other hand, the Japanese feel that when Americans make nearly impossible demands, the Japanese, at a loss for what to do, are then forced to go out into the hall and put their heads together, sometimes placing an emergency long-distance call to headquarters for top-level instructions.

Whatever the reality, both sides feel very uncomfortable about the other's methods. None feels able to communicate with the other on an equal basis.

Most people, Japanese and non-Japanese alike, think that "negotiating skill" refers to an ability to lead talks to a conclusion solely beneficial to one's self. But negotiations are no place for deception, be it one-sided or mutual. To begin with, business talks are not an end in themselves. A successful conclusion is desirable, but insufficient if the relationship deteriorates afterwards.

Tactics aimed at getting one-sided benefits are therefore not a wise course to take. The initial benefits are unlikely to be followed by long-term profits. Like marriage, if one side gains too much, the relationship will not last long. Once this is understood, the art of negotiation begins by ensuring that both sides are fully aware of the goals of the talks and the facts of the case, none of which should be hidden. The facts should then be examined together to reach an agreement in language understood in the same way by both parties. Normally, when talks are said to go badly, it is because the parties have not established a common basis for discussion.

Certainly it will be necessary for Japanese to be more direct. The Japanese approach to negotiations is to skirt the issue again and again, getting gradually closer to the crux of the problem— and the solution. But this approach gives Americans the impression Japanese often have an ulterior motive. They wonder, "Why doesn't he get to the point?"

Japanese businessmen must also learn to list possible solutions at the onset of discussions—to "lay their cards on the table." Then describe how in similar cases in the past a particular solution has or has not worked. This gives an argument the rationalistic wrapping that American businessmen expect.

This is not an easy approach for a Japanese to take. If he used it in Japan and prefaced each discussion with a list of alternatives, he would be thought too self-assertive, pushy, and unpleasant.

The psychological state amenable to persuasion and the mental state of "being persuaded" after a solution to a problem has been found are the same, both in Japan and the United States.

But the way one goes about leading a person from one state to the next differs completely, in terms of both the inputs and the process. To work effectively in America, Japanese will have to face issues more explicitly and draw up alternatives within a rational framework.

Assume that the purpose of the talks is a technical tie-up by which technologies belonging to an American and a Japanese firm will be cross-licensed. Ideally, both sides want to acquire the other side's most advanced technology and should be willing to provide their own most advanced technology in exchange.

In this situation, it is not a good policy to try to substitute one's second best. The reason is simply that the tie-up will flounder if commercialization of the technology provided to the other side is unsuccessful. The outcome will be all the more unacceptable if access is cut off to outside technology that one's own company has successfully commercialized. Technology is evolving rapidly, and firms must build up lasting ties that enable them to obtain the next generation of technology as well and as quickly as possible. In sum, the best course in negotiations is to play the game fairly and in good faith.

The inability to communicate is a very human failing. Unfortunately, these individual failings have global repercussions because the companies of Japan and the United States are often economic superpowers. Joint ventures fail, as a result, and talks about semiconductors or textiles lead to superficial solutions that have to be revised. We may think that we are negotiating, but most of the time we are not even talking the same language.

Japan's Role in Asia

The Japanese believe that they understand Southeast Asians and vice versa. After all, we share the same heritage and have the same skin color. But we should bear in mind that despite the geographical proximity, most Asian countries are quite different from Japan.

Most are former colonies: Indonesia, of the Netherlands; Malaysia, Singaporc, and Hong Kong, of Great Britain; the Philippines, first of Spain, then of the United States. Thus, although they are geographically a part of Asia, the majority of Southeast Asians have a mentality with a far deeper Western tinge than Japan. Even Korea and Taiwan, although former Japanese colonies, have been very significantly influenced, materially and militarily, by the United States, and look to it for models and aid rather than to Japan.

The Southeast Asian approach to things is dry and pragmatic, even calculating—not emotional like that of the Japanese. It is therefore a big mistake to believe that lengthy parleying among Asians will automatically produce understanding. Japan has the same difficulties communicating with the rest of Asia as it does with the United States.

Western culture has changed certain aspects of Asian life. Asian countries were invaded by television and the values it conveys before they had firmly established their own modern cultural foundations. As a result, there is a dangerous imbalance between the ability to create wealth and the demand for it. The

Asians' desire for enjoyment is usually much stronger than their will to earn and learn. They want money and they want to be overnight successes.

Except in Korea and Taiwan, schooling has not been treated as a top priority, and educational levels are relatively low. In some countries, not all shop foremen can add four-digit figures. When the Japanese build a plant in these countries, they must overcome a tremendous education—and expectations—gap. Being very Americanized in their way, the Asians believe in the American dream, and expect considerable monetary awards. As soon as they learn to add four-digit figures and become foremen, they want a private office and a car, something even a Japanese *bucho* (department head) would hesitate to ask for.

Korea has too few universities, and particularly lacks the capacity to train engineers. It will have major problems when it stops borrowing technology from abroad and tries to start innovating on its own, because of the country's critical shortage of engineers. Also, Korea has only a 9 percent savings rate; in the early 1960s, when the Japanese were earning the equivalent of what Koreans earn today, the savings rate in Japan was 20 to 25 percent.

The elite of Asian countries are often schooled in the United States or England. Their mental world is completely westernized, with Japan playing no part in it. That is why it was a big surprise to everyone when Malaysia's Prime Minister Mahathir announced the "Looking East" policy, namely looking to Japan and perhaps Korea, for models.

LEADERSHIP THROUGH MARKET OPENING

Then what sort of relations should Japan seek to have with Asian countries? It must build up ties that enable Asia truly to count on Japan's presence. This can be done by opening its markets.

Japan gave $4.3 billion in aid last year to the Philippines, Thailand, and other countries, in a form known as ODA (office development assistance). It corresponds to .35 percent of GNP, a number higher than that for the U.S. (.24 percent). Our government says that we need to do this to fulfill our responsibilities as a developed nation. But the Malaysians, the Thais, the Filipinos, and the Indonesians have a strong sense of pride, and gratitude for this sort of aid ends as soon as the aid stops. We should learn from the (bitter) experience of the United States in Latin America. Simple aid does not produce friendship. If Japan sincerely intends to become a better friend of Asia, gifts of aid and subsidies must give way to access for Asian products to Japan's vast markets.

It is not enough for Japan to let in more of the raw materials that it has always imported. It should also let secondary goods replace its primary commodity imports from Asia. Instead of lumber, Japan should import furniture from the Philippines; instead of palm oil, it should import detergents and salad oil from Thailand; instead of rubber, it should import tires from Malaysia.

Sole dependence on primary commodity exports is inherently risky, since changes in the business climate cause violent fluctuations in the international primary commodity market. A shift to semifinished and finished products would enable Southeast Asian countries both to promote their domestic industry and to raise their education level and standard of living.

The switch from primary to secondary exports would also be beneficial because it would make the parties more aware of each other. The export of raw materials does not require or stimulate concern by suppliers about conditions in the importing country, but the export of manufactured goods is impossible without an understanding of markets and consumer preferences. Attempts by Asian countries to understand Japan and Japanese consumers will certainly improve our relations.

DO UNTO US AS WE DID TO THE UNITED STATES

Japanese should bear in mind that the American market is currently flooded with imports from most of Asia. The flow of Korean, Malaysian, and Taiwanese goods into the United States makes the openness of its market to these countries indisputable. If Japan were to open its markets to these countries to at least the same extent, it would be releasing the United States in part from its role (some would say its burden) as the market of entry for these developing nations. Naturally, doing so will harm Japanese light industry, but remember that Japan did exactly the same thing to America not so long ago.

The concept of a Triad strategy leaves room for regional responsibilities and opportunities. These are families of developing countries in the economic sphere of each Triad member. Japan has Southeast Asia, the United States has Latin America, and Europe has the Middle East and Africa as historical and geographical partners. Relations between these developed and developing countries—the so-called North-South problem—have in recent years grown worse as the distance between the haves and the have-nots has increased. One of the best ways to make the gap between North and South narrower would be for Japan to switch progressively to higher-value-added industries and leave the production of less-value-added goods to other Asian countries. This would mean shared prosperity, because those involved in high-value-added production still need the items Southeast Asia could produce.

Naturally, abandoning primary and secondary industries would be opposed because domestic industries are certain to suffer.[1] Extra efforts would have to be made to persuade the commonwealth of the benefits that would result.

Technical cooperation between Japan and Asia is one aspect of these relations that has already run into trouble. Some potential participants in technology transfers fear that it will boomerang on cooperating industries in the advanced countries. When, for example, a chemical plant is exported to a developing country, it increases the number of competitors. Domestic companies therefore shy away from technical cooperation, saying, "Why should we give them a knife to stab us in the back?" They also agree that domestic demand cannot be expected to grow any further and that plants should not be built to expand domestic capacity. This consensus is robbed of effect, however, by the fact that, in the chemical industry, the engineering sector is independent of production. Chemical manufacturers can say no, but if engineering firms say yes, plants are exported regardless. The result is that Japanese-built chemical plants in the developing countries are producing ammonia and ammonium sulfate and preventing Japan from exporting these products to overseas markets.

We can't stop the inevitable flow of certain industries away from Japan, just as the United States couldn't. Labor-intensive

---

[1]Approximately 1.4 million more people will be unemployed if Japan completely opens its markets, bringing the unemployment rate to 3.8 percent.

production is already rare in Tokyo; producers in need of cheap labor seek it in the provinces. Some people have lost their jobs in Tokyo in the process, but new jobs have been created in services and new industries. As a result, Tokyo is more prosperous than before.

When things proceed to the next stage, however, and plants move across national borders—for example, from Japan to somewhere in Asia—society begins to put a brake on the process.

It is time for Japan to internationalize its part of the Triad. In the final analysis, economic necessity dictates what ought to be produced where total cost of production is the cheapest. Industry may try to stem the flow of technology, but the current cannot be stopped. Instead of blocking the current, Japan should harness it to power the transition toward higher-value-added industries.

RETREAT FROM ASIA TO AMERICA

But we are doing just the opposite. About a decade ago, labor costs accounted for nearly 25 percent of the costs of production of typical assembly line finished goods. Production costs could therefore be cut by about 20 percent by going somewhere else in Southeast Asia, where labor costs were one fourth the Japanese level. Reexport to American and similar markets was a profitable proposition—then.

It is different today. Higher technology has taken over Japanese industry. In most of Southeast Asia, key high-tech components—microprocessors, video tape recorder cylinder heads—cannot be domestically produced. They must be imported from Japan. Only final assembly is possible. True, in Taiwan many components can now be procured locally, but even in relatively advanced Korea, Japanese parts are needed to build office automation and high-quality photographic, video, and audio equipment. Even less can be done locally in Malaysia and Singapore.

Key components now account for most of the cost of production. Workers' wages (the so-called direct labor costs) now amount to only 7 or 8 percent of total production costs. Halving direct labor costs that are only 8 percent to start with means a mere 4 percent cost reduction. This is not a savings at all, when you consider that the parts must be shipped to the plant and the products must be insured and shipped from the plant to the market. These costs amount to between 14 percent and 15 percent of the price of the finished product.

Finally, the cost of Asian labor is rising. The differential with respect to Japan is rapidly shrinking. Workers in most Southeast Asian countries get average monthly wages in the neighborhood of $300 to $400, about half the Japanese level. It is not necessarily better to go to countries where labor is cheaper than this, either, because of labor productivity problems.

These changes have led most Japanese firms either to bring their plants back to Japan and automate as much as possible, or to produce directly in the main market, North America or Europe, in response to protectionist pressures and possible currency re-alignments. Ten years ago, for example, most of the downstream processes in semiconductor manufacture were handled in Malaysia, the Philippines, and elsewhere in Southeast Asia. Today, only Malaysia still makes a good showing at the labor-intensive low end of semiconductor assembly. Japanese direct investment in ASEAN has been dwindling over the past decade, while direct investment in North America has grown correspondingly.

The United States has already felt the future catching up with it. It still has many labor-intensive assembly line industries whose methods and processes in manufacturing have not changed much in the last 10 to 15 years. A straightforward calculation shows cheap Southeast Asian labor to be advantageous, especially because unions are strong in most parts of the United States. In fact, there is a strong tendency to move plants overseas simply to get away from the unions.[2]

The pattern is increasingly clear. On the one hand, Japan keeps its markets closed and invests its industrial capital pref-

---

[2]They are not doing this indiscriminately. Well-managed American companies now realize that in a country without an adequate infrastructure and supply of components, cheap labor can be very expensive, especially if that cheap labor tends to be displaced and moves from company to company. Companies like Digital Equipment Corporation take a more sophisticated approach. For example, a DEC official had the following to say about sourcing: "The approach of our organization is that competitive advantages go far beyond just cost. We need to look at markets, the quality of the labor force, service, networking, delivery. All those things contribute to a competitive advantage. Whereas companies that just chase after the cheapest production are always chasing it." (Source: "Superior Products May Be U.S. Trade Deficit Solution," *Los Angeles Times*, September 22, 1986, p. 1.)

erentially in the United States. On the other hand, the United States continues to invest in Asia, and opens its vast markets to Asian products, increasing interdependence and benefits for both sides. The Japanese retreat from Asia has reversed in some industries recently, because of the yen's appreciation. Sanyo, for example, just announced that it planned to move 70 percent of its semiconductor output to foreign bases, possibly South Korea or Taiwan. But these are not systematic efforts. They are opportunistic criss-crossing of national borders by companies trying to cope with sudden currency fluctuations. What is lacking is a more fundamental and firm commitment to overseas operations.

Despite the pullback by Japanese companies, there remain good possibilities for Southeast Asian imports to Japan. Textiles, plywood, rubber, footwear, and electric household appliances are among them. This will mean considerable dislocation for our workers, only 13 percent of whom are employed in internationally competitive industries. The price of global citizenship will not be cheap.

The Japanese government decided some years ago to no longer support domestic coal mining, because it cost too much and the coal was of such poor quality that it couldn't even be used in steel mills. As a result, 400,000 miners lost their jobs. But it was the right decision. If Japan had continued to shore up its uncompetitive coal, we would still be paying the price, like several countries in Europe. In England, miners' strikes seemed to be an annual event, with frequent bloody rioting. Agriculture in some other European countries employs 20 percent of the population— and claims 80 percent of the national budget.

Assuming that we live in a free society and that supplies of essential commodities will not be interrupted, protectionism is unnecessary and counterproductive. In a free trade economy, the best companies, whatever their nationality, deserve to survive if they defeat their competition. The best firms take the best course of action and provide the best services to users. Assuming open competition, some companies will go under, and others will rise to the top, and through their dynamism, the nation will prosper. When the basis for competition is unfairly skewed, however, more products are shoddy and wasteful of resources, and vested interests throw their weight around.

Assuming, as I suggested, that competitive Korean textiles entered the Japanese market: Should the Japanese textile industry simply squat dumbly on its haunches and await its fate, like a hog in the stockyard?

Look at what some American textile mills did: When they saw the Japanese coming, Burlington Industries, Textron, and other firms began to upgrade and diversify their products, moving into fashion, carpets, and hi-tech areas new to them. They succeeded and survived. Any company can do this, if it accurately senses consumer trends and moves in the same direction. Conversely, a firm in decline is one whose products either no longer satisfy consumers or cost too much. Such a firm has already begun to lose ground; its demise is simply a question of time, whether competitors arrive from abroad to put it out of business or not.

Japan spends twice as much per capita as the United States on aid to developing countries. It has lavished official development aid on Asia, but that is why it has been unable to increase its leadership there. The postwar American example (especially in Latin America) should make it obvious that no amount of aid to the developing countries will win their support, their hearts, or even their gratitude. If Japan truly wishes to become a leading power in Asia, it has no choice but to open its doors to Asian manufactured goods.

New Vistas, New Challenges

Even in this global age, the Japanese still want their country to be self-sufficient in everything. These feelings are rooted in sentiment and history, and are hard to change.

For centuries, Japan was closed to the rest of the world and by definition self-sufficient. When Japan thrust itself back into the world community, the policies of the Meiji era (1868–1913) were premised on war: "A strong army for a rich nation." This, too, meant self-sufficiency in food and materials. Almost totally lacking in natural resources, Japan struggled for decades with the Herculean task of feeding its population. The key to its achievement was getting the Japanese to work fanatically and educating them to put their nation above every other consideration.

As a result, Japan escaped being colonized and managed to become a major industrial nation. Without doubt, its success was due to the national strategy handed down from the Meiji era. But that strategy can no longer work. This myopia has driven Japan to two wars, World War II and the recent "trade wars." Our ancestors have proven that this route to self-sufficiency leads to misery for everyone.

If there is any way to achieve security in our age, it is by ensuring the free trade of goods between Japan and the world. The more economically interdependent we become, the more unlikely are disruptions. Our implicit assumption of "Japan ver-

119

sus the World" persists, at least in our own mind. We are painting ourselves into a corner of the world, and many of us remain unaware of this. It is hard to say which is more trying, our innocence or our arrogance. Whichever the case, Japan-born-and-bred Japanese must make serious efforts to correct their worldview.

We will not change unless we recognize that we are a rich nation. In Keynes's day, the population was a burden because it had to be fed. Industry was a means to create employment and feed the population. It required natural resources; ergo, those who had natural resources produced and possessed wealth. Today in the Triad, where GNP has reached $10,000 per capita, the fraction of income spent on food has dropped from four fifths to an almost insignificant three tenths. Seven tenths remain for discretionary consumption. All over the advanced world, industries have begun to create greater wealth by focusing on that 70 percent.

Furthermore, Keynes's equation assumes economic activity balanced in a closed national economy. Today the forces behind employment, money supply, demand, and consumption flow across natural borders. If the American government increases its money supply and if there is no need for it there, we see it in Tokyo's money trading counters within a day. If American people want to consume, despite poor supply, our factories get busy. We have to recognize that the world is now completely interlinked. We cannot simply grow in a vacuum. We have to adopt the right perspective that permits us to breathe, literally, the same air as the rest of the world—as the Chernobyl incident painfully demonstrates. Our wishful thinking about special minds is nothing but a myth, but our mental isolation is a real barrier.

Our economists and experts have yet to notice this major change in Japan's fortunes. Because natural resources used to be the key determinant of national power and their absence a critical weakness for Japan, they still think in these terms. But today, the major industrial nations are shifting from material- to immaterial-based, hardware- to software-oriented economies. Increasingly, wealth is the product of advanced knowledge industries, high technology, and complex software systems. These are areas where Japan can excel.

Japan has 120 million units of this most valuable resource, the Japanese people, who have the training needed to function efficiently in an advanced industrial society. Japan's educated and affluent population is an engine of wealth and a huge consumer market for high-value-added goods. Japan is a human resource superpower comparable to, if not greater than, the United States.

In other words, Japan has the key to success in the 21st century. It has everything necessary to respond to whatever might happen, even if its economy were totally liberalized, opened and unprotected. There would be no serious problems. We must recognize this. For if we persist in our ignorance of our transformation from a have-not to a rich nation and fail to escape from our post-war, poor-boy mentality, we will be shunned by other nations, who will belong to a new, interdependent economic order.

REASSESSMENT OF OUR ECONOMIC UNDERPINNINGS

This does not mean Japan can afford a four-day workweek and longer vacations, as many foreign and even domestic experts advise. Maybe America can afford to do this. We cannot. The United States is rich in natural resources to begin with. Its territories are vast enough to feed itself and much of the rest of the world, too. It possesses more oil than any other country, Saudi Arabia included. It has practically everything it needs within its own borders. The United States, more than any other, is a country that can withstand scarcity when the rest of the world is in distress. The point is that the United States has become the world's worst debtor nation and this suggests that national wealth cannot be created automatically from what is given in a nation's soil and earth.

Japan is placed in exactly the opposite situation. Japan cannot rely solely on its own domestic assets. It still relies today on its import and export trade, and the resulting surplus that provides the money to buy food and other resources. Our economy continues to be dependent on processing trade. In this respect the credo taught by school textbooks of my day is still correct.

Over the past 20 to 30 years, there have been significant changes in the pattern of trade and we have become people rich. The creation of value-added is certainly far more important than the value of processed natural resources. At the same time, however, it is also certain that the fundamentals on which our economy operates have not changed. Thus, even though indolence may be permissible in a rich country, in Japan it will have immediate repercussions on our economic foundations. As long as Japan relies on human resources for its survival, it cannot afford any erosion of its human potential.

We must understand this. We must help the world, particularly our critics, understand this. And we must act according to our principles. Americans say our trade is imbalanced, despite a balance in market accessibility. These assertions should be challenged firmly with facts. We should, on the other hand, admit our faults and open our markets to the unstable economies of Southeast Asia. We must balance our trade with these countries. Since none of them have strong enough companies to produce locally in Japan, they find themselves placed in a situation completely different from the United States. Our export surplus with respect to the majority of Asian countries is too great to ignore.

We cannot redress this problem with cavalier give-aways. Japan has reached the stage where it ought to take all of Asia into consideration and be much more conscious of the needs of other countries in general.

Japan now imports palm oil, rubber, and other raw materials from developing countries. This arrangement has led to prosperity for Japan's food and tire industries, and some of the benefits should naturally be distributed among the developing countries.

It is thus not a time to be complacent. Rather it is time to create a new self-image that reflects our strengths and our prospects for the future. That new self-image will be the basis for valuable contributions to the developing world. We can exercise active nonmilitaristic world leadership in many areas. The problem is not to choose where to begin; it is to choose to begin.

Japan should work toward two goals: an economic one that will ensure its survival at a modest level of affluence and another that will create pride in Japan's role in the global community. The latter in particular must generate an image of Japan that is acceptable to our young people and inspire effort toward its realization. For Japan to continue to improve its status internationally, new ideals are needed that will help to maintain our economic foundations as well as turn the younger generation toward personal and national advancement as a desirable goal.

A NEW ECONOMIC ORDER

Two developments have greatly limited the usefulness of Keynesian economics. First, as we have seen, the world economy is far more dynamic today than it was in Keynes's era, when the economic sphere was a composite of closed national units. The world economy is now a much larger system of interdependent units. Demand and production are no longer contained within single national economies. An item produced in a developing nation may be in demand only in the advanced nation.

Second, both productivity and profitability in the advanced countries often increase with a *decrease* in the number of people involved in production. Robots have become agents in economic models.

The age is over when suppliers automatically made profits if they operated in a market where demand was greater than supply. Today, the difficulty lies not in supplying goods but in creating demand. Profits from commodities (be they corn or memory chips) arise only occasionally and in circumscribed geographical locations when demand surges in response to a temporary insufficiency in supply. To make profits continuously, there must be a need for a differentiated product and service.

The production of commodities that anyone can make will increasingly take place in the developing countries, where there is an abundant low-cost labor force. And when labor-intensive industry begins to move to the developing countries, the need for an industrial labor force will gradually disappear in the advanced nations. Keynes's general theory—that demand increases when the business climate improves, necessitating an increase in production, which in turn leads to higher employment—does not apply. Keynes's equation does not take into account the machine variable either. Furthermore, the Keynesian equation of the economy is balanced by the existence of a closed market. The economies of almost every country in the world, however, and especially of the advanced nations, consist of one part that is inextricably connected to all others in addition to another part (their closed markets) that functions independently. This is the main reason for the discrepancy between the Keynesian model and economic reality today. Unfortunately, there is no general model to account for the connecting media uniting the world economy. Adjustments are therefore made bilaterally, with almost no lasting effect.

Today, most advanced nations are in a position where their corporate financial picture would improve if it were permissible to increase unemployment. Firms could make more profits if they replaced people with machines, lowered their personnel costs, and raised their productivity. The increased profits they made could be recycled through taxation or private investment.

But a cycle premised on the permissibility of increased unemployment is one that is likely to be disrupted. It is another area where the concepts guiding the economies of the three Triad regions differ from those of the developing countries, which are largely based on labor-intensive industry.

Not many economists espouse Keynes's theory as he originally proposed it. Lacking a viable alternative framework, we nevertheless find ourselves still unconsciously susceptible to his teachings. Politicians continue to interpret recent phenomena in terms of his theory of the relationship between unemployment and the business cycle. Hence the link that turns unemployment, a natural economic phenomenon, into a political issue.

Politicians also misunderstand the realities of trade "wars." If one examines the relatively low levels of market penetration by foreign firms, then it becomes clear that the biggest reason for unemployment is the existence of powerful domestic firms, their head-to-head competition and (often) resultant overcapacity. Misunderstanding this reality, politicians link unemployment to trade and turn trade into a political issue. To solve the problem of the business cycle and unemployment, we must treat employment as a matter affecting not single countries, but the entire OECD market, and necessitating simultaneous international implementation of coordinated policies. Many Americans would like to curl up and watch old Westerns on television and make cars for themselves. Their dreams of the days when isolation was possible are false dreams. And so are ours.

STRATEGIC THINKING ABOUT RICE

Japanese trading company representatives visiting California on business often come home lugging a large bag of locally grown rice. Although the Japanese generally turn up their noses at non-Japanese rice, trading company gourmets go out of their way to get California and Arkansas rice. They think it tastes good—and it costs only one fifth as much as Japanese rice.

But the Japanese gasp in disbelief when I predict that the United States is likely to urge Japan to buy American rice once the debates about the beef and oranges have been settled.

"You've got to be kidding!" they say, and refuse to believe me, simply because rice is of such dietary and symbolic importance to the Japanese. They assume Americans are at least aware that rice is more than just food to us. That rice is the staff of life to the Japanese. That Japanese are far more sentimentally attached to it than the Americans are to bread or the Italians to pasta. Would the United States ask Italy, they say, to import American spaghetti?

But to a farmer in Arkansas, rice is just another crop—sources of carbohydrate that hardly differ. If there's a market for soy beans, he'll plant soy. If wheat sells, he'll plant wheat. And if people will buy rice, he'll plant rice. Americans cannot even imagine that the Japanese feel as strongly about rice as they do. And that's only to be expected; we have not made any effort to explain how we feel to Americans.

What happens if we attempt to analyze rice, with its potential for escalating into the next unpleasant bilateral issue, using a completely different transnational approach? First of all, we know that there is not much chance of turning the current rice price support deficit into a surplus. The Japanese government buys rice from farmers and sells it to distributors at less than cost. The ruling political party just agreed to keep prices at the same level as last year. Until current policies are changed, there is no way both to guarantee the livelihoods of Japanese farmers and to make more money from rice sales than is spent on purchases. Usable land in Japan is critically limited and as long as paddies are farmed domestically, there will be a deficit.

But Japan could grow its rice in the United States, or for that matter, in Australia, letting farmers in Japan control its distribution and sale. If Japan spent an amount equivalent to the rice price support deficit for only two years, that is, $8 billion, it could buy land in the fertile grain belts of Arkansas and California equal in area to Japan's total paddy acreage. The third year, there would be no more deficit, and rice could be bought at less than half the current price.

As farfetched as it may sound, this strategy for finding a structural solution to the agricultural price support deficit has a good chance of succeeding, provided the nation is viewed as a sort of macroenterprise. The national interest would shift in the people's favor because Japan and the United States would have closer shared interests from the moment that Japanese owned land in the United States, gave jobs to local farmers, and farmed and paid taxes on the crops they grew. As owners of farms and employers of American farmers, Japanese would acquire a measure of influence on public opinion and be a more legitimate participant in the U.S. economy. Land ownership, we must recognize, can be as sensitive a matter in U.S. agriculture as rice is to the Japanese, so this solution must be approached thoughtfully.

This strategy would certainly be subject to suspicions of a political nature at home. People would be alarmed at the reduction in Japan's self-sufficiency in food. Others would ask for guarantees that the United States would not cut off access to our rice paddies in the event of a crisis. (Remember Nixon's embargo of soy products to Japan during his China shock days.)

But the world political and economic situation is too complex to allow a confrontation with Japan immediately to become a food blockade. The argument can even be turned around as with the United States and machine tools; the more inextricably interwoven our interests, the greater our mutual security.

Today, our society is already globalizing at a dizzying pace, and tomorrow the process will continue. The course for natural-resourceless Japan can only be found, I believe, in resolutely taking the lead in internationalization. Already, some of Japan's best and biggest enterprises are doing just this, moving into world markets and expanding to the most distant corners of the globe as if national borders did not exist.

A NEW PERSPECTIVE FOR A NEW WORLD

Myths and misperceptions cloud Japan's view on many issues. The world misunderstands Japan, and Japan misunderstands the world. These misunderstandings have spawned conflicts everywhere.

The more we examine the circumstances, the more we find that our conflicts are based on illusions while our true interests are actually in close alignment. This realization should, but in reality doesn't, provide the basis for dialogue.

The problem lies in the way we have allowed democracy to deviate from its ostensible purpose of providing the greatest good for the greatest possible number. The world's democracies are not putting this dictum into practice.

In the name of democracy, our nations are being overly responsive to special interests. Their problems are always given considerable, often excessive attention. We respect their rights as a democratic principle, but go too far when we turn those rights into subsidies and protection.

It is a mistake to view economic friction in terms of conflicts or trade wars. The fact is that conflicts between countries tend to be alleviated by transfers of goods and movements of people. Fierce competition may cause some firms to collapse and others to succeed, but the benefits and losses in the end are likely to be evenly divided. Within a country, the weakest are normally eliminated by natural selection, approved usually by a consensus of consumers. But in international competition, subconscious patriotism surfaces and complicates the issues, although a strong country should be in no danger of having its firms succumb to outside competition.

In Japan, farmers, 6 percent of the population, have 18 percent of the votes and 25 percent voting influence as they vote more regularly than urban workers. Their influence and the resulting unfair protection of farm products forces the remaining 94 percent of the population, the vast majority, to put up with prolonged, senseless international conflict.

We would have much more residential land on which to build spacious houses if half our land were not used unproductively to cultivate rice. The inability of the government to cope with the rice problem forces us to pay dearly for cramped lodgings in houses built practically eave to eave. We're rich in play money, but live as if we are poor.

The reforms that would solve these problems are difficult but not impossible to implement. There is no reason why we cannot achieve in Japan what Belgians and Dutch have managed to do despite much greater population densities.

LOOK OUTWARD

The rubber harvesters in the jungle are human beings who sweat and toil for a little over a dollar a day. Yet their labor is the foundation of a Japanese industry. Much of the squid served at sushi bars in Tokyo is caught by fishermen in Madagascar. The tomatoes that go into ketchup come from Portugal and Taiwan. Japan's butter comes from Australia and New Zealand.

Instead of telling our children to thank Japan's farmers for their food, we should teach them to thank the world's farmers and fishermen. That is probably the first step toward building awareness of ourselves as world citizens.

Japan's economic sphere is broadening to encompass the whole world. Shamefully, however, we feel no need to be grateful for what we get from outside Japan. Let's begin to share the peace and wealth we enjoy with the world, because our country cannot survive in isolation. Especially not in the 21st century.

Our biggest problem is that we cannot see beyond our borders. Our shortsightedness is preventing us from becoming full-fledged members of a much greater world community.

The Apollo 7 astronaut Wally Schirra once said that the thing that impressed him most about looking at the earth from outer space was that the borders between countries weren't visible. National borders are virtually meaningless today. In our new economic system, cooperation and interdependence, not conflict and independence, are prerequisites for survival. If only we can dispel our illusions, wake up to the truth, and broaden our perspective, we'll see a whole new world before us.